Georgian Bay Gourmet

Winter Entertaining

Written by: Anne Connell
             Helen DeCarli
             Mary Hunt
             Jean Leavens
             Anne Parker

Published by: Georgian Bay Gourmets' Publishing Ltd.
               307-5th Street, Midland, Ontario L4R 3W7

Edited by: Eric Mundinger
            and Barbara Hacker

Photographs by: Hudson Leavens

Flowers by: Perrin's, Midland, Ontario

First printing, August 1980
Second printing, November 1980
Third printing, March 1981
Fourth printing, May 1982

Printed by Southam Murray Printing,
2973 Weston Road, Weston, Ontario, Canada

Graphics & Design by Raesgo
Barrie, Ontario, Canada

Musson Book Company
A Division of General Publishing Co. Limited
Toronto, Canada

Canadian Cataloguing in Publication Data

   Title: Georgian Bay Gourmet
      Winter Entertaining

   Includes Index

   ISBN 0-9690361-0-8

   1. Cookery   I. Title   II. Gourmet Recipes

Introduction

We are a group of five women. Each of us is proud of our individual contributions to this book; however, our work as a group—the sharing and blending of our many ideas—has proved to be both rewarding and invaluable. We agreed wholeheartedly at the onset that you can't be a good cook without a sense of humour and a glass of wine, and it was usually this which kept our project from curdling or turning sour! So often our most vital ingredient was a good laugh to smooth out our problems, resulting in a delightfully rich experience.

Amongst us we have delivered ten children. One of us is a single-parent, while another was married 14 years before she had her child. Three of us are full-time workers, while two of us have retired from the working world to raise our families. Three of us live in the town of Midland; two of us live outside the town on the shores of Georgian Bay. None of us was born here; one was raised here; one of us is French. One of us is a qualified nurse but is now a practising real estate agent. One of us travels extensively throughout the province giving workshops on counselling to those involved in social services. One of us was a librarian several years ago, while another spent a year in Toronto working with wayward street kids. One of the group is a medical secretary, while another is the president of the Huronia Association for the Mentally Retarded; one woman is devoted to bringing Children's Theatre to this area. There is one member who has lived in Malaysia and has travelled throughout South East Asia and Africa, while three of us have journeyed extensively in Britain and Continental Europe; one woman lived in England for two years. And, a few years ago, two of us travelled down the Colorado River in a rubber raft!

Our experiences have varied but we have a number of things in common. First, we all take pride in the unique qualities of the Georgian Bay area and in what it has to offer to the rest of Ontario and Canada. Second, we enjoy a Georgian Bay winter and we all take part in either cross-country skiing, skating or snowmobiling. Third, and probably most important, each of us enjoys cooking, entertaining and eating. We combined these interests with our friendship and adventure-some spirits, and ended up with this book.

We would like to thank Gary Westgarth who brought us together for this project, and who survived our crazy lunchtime meetings where we discussed never-fail pastry along with the pros and cons of natural childbirth! Our thanks also to our families and friends for their understanding and continued support during the many hours of work which went into this publication. We shall always be grateful to those who shared our enthusiasm and believed in the value of, and the people behind, this book. Most of all, we thank each other for those incredibly funny moments which we will never forget!

HED

Table of contents

This book is written as an entertainment guide
for the long winter months particular to the Georgian Bay
Area. Each chapter contains activities and recipes in menu form to
complement the season. In a few chapters we present groups of additional
recipes using those foods which are common to the time of year.
Included also is a section which deals with some Basic
Preparations, a Vegetable Cooking Chart, and
Cooking Terms used for the purpose of this book.
Good reading . . . good eating.

The Metric Question

Our cookbook is not in metric measure because we feel your favourite soufflé or cake is a chemically balanced formula and therefore should be professionally adjusted to metric measurements. There are no direct conversions for such measurements as ⅓ of a cup or ½ a teaspoon. A properly developed metric recipe will call for easier to measure amounts of 250 mL or 500mL instead of the direct conversion for 1 cup which would be 237 mL. When you employ such measurements, the recipes are not reliable.

Continue to use your old recipes the way they are but buy metric measuring equipment and try *new* metric recipes. Do not spend time converting. The Metric Commission of Canada has suggested the use of benchmarks initially in learning metric and we have listed some of these.

250 mL	Replaces 8 oz. cup
15 mL	Replaces 1 tbsp.
5 mL	Replaces 1 tsp.
5 cm	is about 2 inches
1 kg	is a little more than 2 pounds
500 g	is a little more than 1 pound
100°	water boils
160°	325°
180°	350°
190°	375°
1 L	pie plate — 9 x 1½″
2 L	cake pan — 8″ square
4 L	cake pan — 13 x 9″ rectangular
1.2 L	layer cake pan — 8 x 1½″ round

Autumn

Chapter One: Autumn

Autumn

In Autumn the Georgian Bay countryside is ablaze with glorious colour. The farmers' fields are full of pumpkins, and the sound of rustling leaves can be heard as children run through the parks. Autumn is also the season of harvest, and the time for Thanksgiving. The family gets together to share the end of the good weather, perhaps the last of the boating or a hike through a colourful Huronia forest, and always the traditional Thanksgiving dinner.

But don't forget, it's Fall Fair time! Now is the time to display the fruits (and vegetables) of your labours. The Coldwater Fall Fair has been running for more than eighty years and is a good example of community involvement. There you will see a wide variety of exhibits and displays including livestock entries and field and garden produce. It is always fun to support this type of event, and to enter some of your own efforts. Who knows, maybe your pickles wil win first prize—ours once did!

This is also a good time of year to visit the Collingwood and Meaford areas where apples, fresh cider, apple butter and hot apple pie can be purchased at roadside stands. There is nothing like the flavour of a fresh Georgian Bay apple and due to their abundance in the fall we have included several apple recipes for your enjoyment.

Another popular fall event is "Octoberfest" which is welcomed by the many German-Canadian citizens of the Georgian Bay region. Each weekend hosts a beer festival in one town or another, and these celebrations usually consist of lots of delicious food, a hearty round of um-pah-pahs, and good old-fashioned fellowship.

Many of our friends look forward to Autumn to once again subscribe to a season of the Huronia Players, a group which has presented live theatre of the highest quality for the last 18 years. People get together for one of the "Players" performances, followed by a post performance dinner to discuss the play. Good eating always complements an evening of entertainment.

The end of October becomes a very exciting time for children. (Hallowe'en reminds them of creative costumes, Jack O'Lanterns, and of course all the candy they can carry.) For a few extra special (but simple) sweet treats, we offer a selection of Hallowe'en recipes, some of which the kids can make themselves.

As warm days turn to cold nights, Autumn turns to winter, and winter brings the Christmas holiday season. It is time to start thinking of those recipes which need extra time to mature. In this chapter we have included a recipe for dark Christmas cake which has been handed down through three generations of a friend's family. When all the ingredients for the cake are combined, each member of the family takes a turn at stirring the pot. The "Big Stir" ensures each participant a year of happiness and good health.

Whether you are tidying up for the summer, or preparing ahead for Christmas, the fall months can be busy, but fun, for all. Do take time out to visit the Georgian Bay area and view the magnificent fall panorama. And, don't forget to combine this glorious season with fine food.

Accent Turkey
(for eight)

Brandied Pumpkin Soup
Roast Turkey With Apple Raisin Stuffing
Snappy Green Beans
Potatoes Julienne
Spiced Acorn Squash
Cranberry Orange Relish
Light and Golden Pumpkin Pie

Brandied Pumpkin Soup
(Serves 8)

¼ cup butter
½ cup finely chopped onion
¼ tsp. ginger
¼ tsp. nutmeg
¼ tsp. allspice

Salt and pepper to taste
3½ cups chicken broth
2 cups prepared pumpkin
1 cup half and half cream
2 tbsp. brandy

- Melt butter in large soup kettle.
- Sauté onions until transparent.
- Add spices and chicken broth and bring to a boil.
- Add pumpkin and cream; heat thoroughly, stirring frequently.
- Stir in brandy and serve.

Serving Suggestion: milk can be used to thin soup if desired.

Roast Turkey With Apple Raisin Stuffing
(Serves 8, Oven 325°)

12 lb. turkey requires 1 recipe Apple Raisin Stuffing.

Apple Raisin Stuffing

1 cup butter or margarine
¾ cup minced onion
1½ cups chopped celery stalks and leaves
7 cups bread crumbs
1 tbsp. salt

1½ tsp. crushed sage leaves
1 tsp. thyme leaves
½ tsp. pepper
3 cups finely chopped apples
¾ cup raisins

- In a large skillet melt butter, add onion and celery and cook until tender.
- Stir in 2 cups of the bread crumbs. Turn into a deep bowl, add remaining ingredients and toss.

Roast Turkey

		Internal Thermometer
8 - 12 lbs.	Cook 3½ - 4½ hours	185°
12 - 16 lbs.	Cook 4½ - 5½ hours	185°

- Rinse turkey cavity with cold water and pat dry.
- Stuff turkey and place breast side up in a shallow roasting pan.
- Brush turkey with oil or butter.
- Insert meat thermometer in thickest part of breast. Roast uncovered in preheated oven, approximately 4½ hours or until thermometer reaches 185°. Baste frequently.

Snappy Green Beans
(Serves 8)

2 lbs. fresh green beans	¼ cup chopped onion
4 slices bacon	2 tbsp. tarragon vinegar

- Cook beans until just tender.
- Fry bacon until crisp and place on paper towelling.
- Sauté onions in bacon fat until tender and add vinegar.
- Drain beans and pour hot vinegar mixture over them. Toss.
- Place in serving dish and crumble bacon over beans.

Potatoes Julienne
(Serves 8)

1 head celery	salt
4 medium potatoes	pepper
1 oz. butter	parsley chopped to garnish
1 small onion finely chopped	

- Clean and trim celery stalks and peel potatoes. Cut into julienne strips (⅛″ thick x 2″ long).
- Keep potatoes in bowl of cold water to keep colour and remove starch.
- Heat butter in pan, add celery and onion. Sauté 4 to 5 minutes. Vegetables should not colour. This can be done well ahead.
- Drain potatoes and dry in cloth.
- Place in pan; add seasonings and stir carefully to blend.
- Cover and cook until potatoes are tender, stirring occasionally (8 to 10 minutes).
- Dust with chopped parsley and serve.

Spiced Acorn Squash
(Serves 8, Oven 325°)

4 medium acorn squash
½ cup dark brown sugar
1 tsp. cinnamon
½ tsp. nutmeg
¼ tsp. cloves

¼ tsp. salt
½ cup melted butter
½ cup maple syrup
about 2 cups boiling water

- Cut each squash in half and remove seeds and fibres.
- In a small bowl cream together brown sugar, cinnamon, nutmeg, cloves, salt and butter.
- Arrange squash in a shallow baking dish just large enough to hold the 8 pieces.
- Spoon an equal amount of spiced butter into each squash and top with a teaspoon of maple syrup.
- Add ½" boiling water to baking dish and bake 1½ hours.

Cranberry Orange Relish
(Yields 1 quart)

½ cup water
½ cup orange juice
1 cup sugar

1 lb. whole cranberries
2 tbsp. orange rind, grated

- In a 4 quart saucepan stir water, juice and sugar together until sugar has dissolved.
- Add berries, bring to a boil and cook stirring occasionally until skins of berries begin to pop (3 to 5 minutes).
- Remove from heat and stir in orange rind.
- Transfer to a serving bowl and chill several hours before serving.

Light and Golden Pumpkin Pie
(Serves 8, Oven 350°)

1 9" pie shell (See Basics, Pg. 212)
2 cups prepared pumpkin
1 cup milk
3 egg yolks beaten
1 cup sugar
½ tsp. cinnamon
⅛ tsp. cloves

⅛ tsp. nutmeg
¼ tsp. ginger
¼ tsp. mace
1 tsp. vanilla
3 egg whites stiffly beaten
1 cup whipping cream, whipped

- Mix pumpkin, milk, egg yolks, sugar, spices and vanilla.
- Fold in the stiffly beaten egg whites.
- Turn mixture into an unbaked pie shell.
- Bake for 45 minutes. Remove from oven and let settle for a few hours.

Serving Suggestion: Dot with dollops of whipped cream when serving.

Vegetarian's Gratitude

(for six)

Ratatouille
Baked Walnut and Cheddar Cheese Béchamel
Marinated Mushrooms
Impossible Pie

Ratatouille

(Serves 6)

1 large onion	4 tbsp. olive oil
1 medium eggplant	1 tsp. basil
2 green peppers	1 cup tomato juice
3 medium zucchini	¾ cup tomato paste
1 cucumber	3 tomatoes
1 small hot red pepper	1 recipe Vinaigrette Sauce (below)
3 cloves garlic	½ cup minced parsley

- Coarsely chop onion; dice eggplant into 1″ cubes; quarter and slice peppers; cut zucchini into ¼″ slices; dice cucumbers; mince hot red pepper; peel garlic cloves and put through garlic press.
- Heat oil in large skillet, add minced red pepper, garlic and basil. Stir fry 2 to 3 minutes and add the onions.
- Stir for a few minutes, add the zucchini, eggplant and the green peppers; toss and stir with two spoons until everything seems to be coated evenly in oil. (Add more oil if vegetables are sticking).
- Mix together the tomato juice and paste; pour over vegetables in skillet and add the cucumbers.
- Cook vegetables slowly in liquid, stirring occasionally until the liquid is almost evaporated (about 1 hour). (Ratatouille should have a little free liquid but still be of a thick consistency, the vegetables should be tender but not falling apart).
- While the mixture is cooking, cut tomatoes into eights and add during last couple of minutes of cooking.
- Chill Ratatouille well. To serve, add Vinaigrette Sauce, and toss lightly. Garnish with parsley.

Vinaigrette Sauce

(Yields ¾ cup)

¼ cup vinegar	½ cup olive oil
1 tbsp. lemon juice	salt and pepper
¼ tsp. mustard	

- Place ingredients in blender and process 15 seconds.

Serving Suggestion: This dish may be served hot; omit vinaigrette sauce.

Baked Walnut and Cheddar Cheese Béchamel
(Serves 6, Oven 375°)

1½ cups ground walnuts
5 oz. grated cheddar cheese
½ cup bread crumbs
½ cup wheat germ
½ cup finely chopped onion

¾ cup milk
2 tbsp. parsley
pepper and salt
2 eggs well beaten
1 recipe Herbed Béchamel Sauce (below)

- In large bowl mix together ground walnuts, cheese, bread crumbs, wheat germ, onions and milk.
- Add parsley, pepper, salt, eggs, and mix.
- Roll mixture into small egg-sized balls and arrange in baking dish. (Makes about 20 balls).
- Pour Béchamel Sauce over balls and bake in oven for 35 to 40 minutes.

Herbed Béchamel Sauce

3 tbsp. butter
1 cup minced onion
3 tbsp. flour
2½ cups hot milk

1 tsp. thyme
salt and pepper
1 tiny bay leaf
nutmeg

- In a double boiler heat butter until bubbly, add onion and cook 3 to 4 minutes over low heat.
- Stir in flour and continue cooking a few more minutes; add milk a little at a time, stirring all the while with a whisk. The sauce will begin to thicken within a few minutes.
- Add thyme, salt and pepper, bay leaf and nutmeg and let mixture cook slowly for 10 to 15 minutes.
- Strain through a sieve.

Marinated Mushrooms
(Serves 6)

1 cup vinegar
¼ cup oil
2 - 3 bay leaves
pinch of thyme

pinch of basil
pinch of oregano
1 clove garlic, minced
1 lb. fresh mushrooms cut in half lengthwise

- Place vinegar and oil in a saucepan; add seasonings and bring to a boil.
- Pour hot liquid over mushrooms.
- Marinate several hours before serving; toss occasionally.

Impossible Pie
(Serves 6, Oven 350°)

4 eggs
½ cup butter
½ cup flour
2 cups milk

1 cup sugar
1 cup coconut
2 tsp. vanilla
1 tsp. nutmeg

- Place all ingredients in blender; process until just blended.
- Place mixture in a well buttered 9″ pie plate.
- Bake for 50 minutes or until set. Cool before serving. Pie usually falls when cool.

Preparation Note: This no crust, one step pie is delicious. The flour forms the crust; eggs, butter and milk form the filling and the coconut makes the topping.

Apple Additions

Applesauce
(Yields 2 - 3 cups)

8 medium apples
½ cup water

¼ cup sugar
1 tsp. cinnamon

Whole Pieces Method:
- Quarter and core apples, pare if desired; place in saucepan.
- Add water; cover and cook slowly until tender.
- Add sugar and cinnamon; continue cooking until sugar dissolves.

Purée Method:
- Cook apples as above. Before adding sugar, press through sieve or colander or place in a blender.
- Return to stove, add sugar. Cook until sugar dissolves.

Apple Cream
(Serves 4 - 6)

1 cup whipping cream, chilled
¼ tsp. vanilla
6 tbsp. sugar

⅓ cup fresh orange juice
2 tbsp. lemon juice
6 large apples

- Beat cream until it starts to thicken; add vanilla and half of the sugar. Beat until cream stands in peaks.
- Combine orange and lemon juice with remaining sugar. Grate peeled apples into juice. (Juice helps to prevent apples from discolouring.)
- Chill mixtures separately. To serve, fold mixtures together.

Apple Fritters
(Yields 2 dozen)

3 - 4 tart apples   1 recipe Batter (below)
                                               icing sugar

- Pare and core apples.
- Slice into ⅛″ rounds to resemble doughnuts.

Batter:

1⅓ cups flour   2 eggs beaten
2 tsp. baking powder   ⅔ cup milk
1 tbsp. sugar   1 tbsp. oil
½ tsp. salt   oil for frying

- Sift dry ingredients together.
- Blend eggs, milk and oil.
- Add dry ingredients all at once to milk mixture and mix until moistened.

To Assemble:

- Dip apple rounds in batter a few at a time.
- Drop coated rounds into deep hot fat (375°). Fry until puffy and golden (3 to 4 minutes), turning once.
- Drain on paper towels. While warm sprinkle with icing sugar and serve at once.

Preparation Note: To keep fritters hot, place them in a slow oven (250°) before sprinkling with sugar.

Harvest Torte
(Serves 6, Oven 400°)

4 cups diced unpared apples   1 cup sugar
½ cup flour   2 tsp. baking powder
1 egg   1 tbsp. melted butter
1 tsp. vanilla   ½ cup broken walnuts
½ cup pitted dates, chopped

- Combine all ingredients and mix thoroughly, but do not beat.
- Turn into greased 8″ x 8″ x 2″ pan.
- Bake in hot oven for 40 minutes.
- Cut into squares.

Serving Suggestion: Nice served with whipped cream.

Tarte Tatin
(Serves 8, Oven 450°)

This is an upside-down version of an open-faced flan.

2¼ cups flour
½ tsp. salt
3 tbsp. sugar
5 oz. butter
1 egg

4 tbsp. cold soda water or ginger ale
7 - 8 large apples
1 recipe Caramel (below)

- In a bowl combine 2 cups flour, salt and sugar.
- Make a well and add butter, egg and soda water or ginger ale.
- Using hands, work in flour from the middle. Gradually work in all the flour. Knead the crust in ¼ cup of flour. Mixture will be sticky.
- Wrap dough in waxed paper and refrigerate one hour.

Caramel:

10 heaping tbsp. white sugar   6 tbsp. cold water

- Warm a deep 10″ pie plate or quiche pan.
- Combine sugar and water in a heavy pan over high heat. Watch carefully but do not stir. Remove from heat when caramel has a dark golden colour.
- Pour hot caramel into heated pie plate, tipping plate so that caramel covers the surface.
- Put aside and roll out pastry.

To Assemble:
- Peel, core and slice apples.
- Arrange apple slices in an attractive pattern over caramel. (Only first layer matters as pie is turned out.)
- The rest of the apples should be piled on top, sprinkle to taste with sugar and dot with butter. Fill dish to top.
- Lay crust on top, pressing the dough inside the edges of pie plate. Prick surface of crust.
- Place in oven and bake 35 to 40 minutes.
- Allow to cool 10 to 15 minutes and invert onto serving plate.

Serving Suggestion: For an added touch, drizzle Calvados or Brandy over tart, and serve with unsweetened whipped cream or Crème Fraîche. (See Basics, page 206).

Cheddar Apple Tart
(Serves 8, Oven 450°)

6 large apples, peeled, cored & sliced
1¼ cup sugar
2 tbsp. lemon juice
1 tsp. vanilla
1⅓ cups flour
1 tsp. salt

½ cup + 1 tbsp. butter
¼ cup ice water
1 tsp. cinnamon
2 cups shredded cheddar cheese
2 - 3 tbsp. brown sugar (if required)

- Combine sliced apples, ½ cup sugar, lemon juice and vanilla in a large bowl. Stir and set aside for 30 minutes.
- Meanwhile, place flour, 1 tbsp. sugar and salt in a bowl.
- Cut in ½ cup butter with a pastry blender.
- Sprinkle ice water over surface, 1 tbsp. at a time and mix lightly with a fork, just until pastry holds together. Shape into a ball and set aside.
- Drain apple slices.
- Butter an 8″ cast iron skillet with remaining tablespoon of butter.
- Sprinkle in remaining sugar.
- Arrange a layer of apples in a circular pattern on bottom of skillet. Sprinkle with ½ tsp. of cinnamon.
- Arrange remaining apples and sprinkle with remaining cinnamon. Press down on apples to compact.
- Sprinkle with cheddar cheese.
- Roll pastry dough to a 10½″ circle. Place on top of cheese and tuck down edges into skillet. Cut steam slits in pastry.
- Place skillet on medium high heat for 5 minutes. Remove from heat.
- Place skillet in oven over a pan to catch drips and bake 30 minutes.
- Return skillet to top of stove and cook on medium high heat for 5 minutes or until liquid around edges evaporates.
- Remove from heat and let stand 5 minutes before turning out onto your serving platter. If sugar has not caramalized sufficiently and platter is heat proof, you can sprinkle on 2 to 3 tbsp. brown sugar and place under broiler for 2 to 3 minutes. Serve warm.

Baked Apples
(Serves 6 - 8, Oven 375°)

6 - 8 large baking apples
1 cup brown sugar
¼ cup butter

cinnamon
1 cup water

- Core apples leaving bottom intact, and pare strip from top of each. Place in baking dish.
- Combine brown sugar and butter. Place some of the mixture in each apple and sprinkle with cinnamon.
- Pour cup of water around apples and bake uncovered for 1 hour. Baste apples several times during baking.

Apple Kuchen
(Serves 8, Oven 375°)

½ cup butter or margarine
1½ cups sugar
2 eggs beaten
1 tsp. vanilla
2 tsp. baking powder

3 cups flour
1 tsp. salt
1 cup milk
4 - 6 medium apples
¼ cup sugar
1 tsp. cinnamon

- Cream butter and sugar.
- Add in eggs and vanilla.
- Mix dry ingredients together in another bowl.
- To butter mixture, add dry ingredients and milk, alternating a little of each at a time. Mix well. (Batter will be thick).
- Pour into greased 13″ x 9″ pan.
- Peel and core apples and cut into wedges. Arrange apple wedges on batter. Poke into dough and sprinkle with ¼ cup sugar and 1 tsp. cinnamon for topping.
- Bake 30 to 40 minutes.

Serving Suggestion: Nice served with light custard.

Apple Chutney
(Yields 3 pints)

6 cups green cooking apples, peeled,
    cored and chopped
2½ cups seedless raisins
2 cups cider vinegar
1 tbsp. mustard seed
2 red peppers, seeded and chopped

3 onions coarsely chopped
2¼ cups brown sugar
1 tsp. salt
dash of cayenne pepper
1 tsp. ginger
1 tsp. pickling spice

- Place all ingredients in a large heavy pot. Simmer uncovered over low heat for 2½ hours, until mixture has thickened. Stir frequently to prevent sticking.
- Pour into hot sterilized jars and seal.

Oktoberfest
(for eight)
Cold Carrot and Tomato Soup
Hot Potato Salad With Bratwurst
Sweet Sour Red Cabbage
Onion Salad
Apple Cake

Cold Carrot and Tomato Soup
(Serves 8)

¾ cup diced onion
¼ cup butter
8 medium carrots, shredded
1 cup orange juice

2 cups stewed tomatoes
salt and pepper
1 cup grapefruit juice
sour cream

- Sauté onion in butter for 1 minute; stir in carrots and sauté over low heat for 2 to 3 minutes.
- Add ½ cup orange juice; cover and cook slowly until the carrots are cooked.
- Add tomatoes and cook for 2 more minutes. Add salt and pepper to taste.
- Purée in batches adding in the rest of the orange juice and grapefruit juice. (If soup is too thick, thin it down with more juice. Use orange juice if a sweeter soup is preferred, or grapefruit juice if a tarter soup is preferred).
- Chill soup.

Serving Suggestion: Serve chilled with dollop of sour cream.

Hot Potato Salad With Bratwurst
(Serves 8)

8 medium potatoes, cooked
4 lb. cooked bratwurst sausage

1 recipe Dressing (below)

- Dice cooked potatoes.
- Slice cooked bratwurst into 1″ slices.
- Keep warm.

Dressing:

1 cup mayonnaise (see Basics, page 206)
1 tsp. celery seed
2 tbsp. vinegar

1 tsp. prepared mustard
½ cup green relish
1 onion, finely chopped

- Combine all ingredients in a saucepan and bring to a low boil, stirring all the while to prevent separation.

To Assemble:
- Combine potatoes and bratwurst in a casserole dish.
- Add dressing and toss. Serve hot.

Sweet Sour Red Cabbage
(Serves 8)

½ cup chopped onion
½ cup butter
1 head red cabbage (2 lb.) shredded
½ cup wine vinegar

¼ cup brown sugar
1 cup water
2¾ cups sliced tart apples
½ tsp. allspice

- In a heavy saucepan, sauté onions in butter.
- Add cabbage and sauté a few minutes.
- Add remaining ingredients and mix well. Bring to a boil and simmer for 1 hour stirring occasionally.

Onion Salad
(Serves 8)

3 large Spanish onions
salt

1 recipe Dressing (below)

- Slice onions very thin and separate into rings. Place in a bowl and sprinkle lightly with salt.

Dressing:

1 cup cider vinegar
1 tsp. pickling spice

1 cup brown sugar

- Combine ingredients and bring to a boil.
- Pour hot mixture over onions and chill thoroughly.

Apple Cake
(Serves 8, Oven 350°)

2 cups whole wheat flour
¼ cup bran flour
2 tsp. baking soda
1 tsp. cinnamon
1 tsp. salt
½ tsp. nutmeg
4 cups diced, peeled tart cooking apples
   (4 large apples)

1 cup sugar
1 cup packed brown sugar
½ cup oil
1 cup chopped walnuts
2 eggs, well beaten
1 tsp. vanilla
3 tbsp. sifted icing sugar

- Stir together flour, bran, soda, cinnamon, salt and nutmeg.
- In a large bowl combine apples, sugars, oil, walnuts, eggs and vanilla.
- Add flour mixture to apple mixture and stir gently with a wooden spoon to blend.
- Turn into a greased 13″ x 9″ x 3″ baking pan. Bake for 50 minutes, or until cake pulls away from the sides of the pan.
- Place pan on rack to cool, sprinkle with sifted icing sugar. Cut into bars.

After The Theatre
(for eight)
Jambalaya
Poppy Seed and Vegetable Salad
Irish Soda Bread
Banana Almond Fool
Lacy Fingers

Jambalaya
(Serves 8)

1 cup chopped onion	pinch cloves
1 clove garlic, minced	½ tsp. thyme
½ cup green peppers, diced	1 tsp. salt
1 cup cooked ham, diced	¼ cup chopped parsley
½ lb. pepperoni, sliced	1 28 oz. can tomatoes
⅓ cup butter	2 cups scallops, rinsed
1½ cups chicken broth	2 lbs. shrimp (shelled & deveined)
pinch nutmeg	3 cups instant rice, uncooked
pinch cayenne	

- In a deep saucepan sauté onions, garlic, green pepper, ham and pepperoni in butter until vegetables are tender.
- Add chicken broth, parsley and tomatoes to vegetable mixture. Bring to a boil and simmer 10 minutes.
- Add scallops and shrimp; simmer 3 minutes.
- Bring to a slow boil and stir in rice.
- Cover and remove from heat, let stand for 5 minutes.

Preparation Note: To prepare ahead, complete all steps up to adding the rice. Remove from heat and refrigerate.
To Serve: Bring mixture to room temperature and complete last 2 steps.

Poppy Seed and Vegetable Salad
(Serves 8, Oven 350°)

Poppy Seed Dressing

⅓ cup vinegar	1 tsp. salt
⅔ cup oil	¼ tsp. pepper
¼ cup sugar	1 tbsp. poppy seeds
1 tsp. dry mustard	2 tbsp. finely minced onion

- Blend all ingredients together.

Salad

3 cups bread cubes	3 cups broccoli flowerets
3 quarts torn assorted salad greens	2½ cups zucchini slices
3 cups cauliflower flowerets	

- Toss bread cubes with ⅓ cup dressing. Bake on a cookie sheet for 20 minutes, turning occasionally.
- Combine remaining ingredients with ⅔ cup dressing (or to taste) in a salad bowl. Add bread cubes and toss lightly.

Irish Soda Bread

(Yields 1 large round, Oven 350°)

2 cups flour	1⅛ tsp. salt
1½ cups whole wheat flour	⅓ cup white or brown sugar
½ cup bran	1½ - 2 cups buttermilk
1⅛ tsp. baking soda	

- Place all dry ingredients in a large bowl, mix together.
- Add buttermilk and mix until mixture is thick and sticky. Form a ball.
- Divide into two small rounds or bake as one larger round. Score tops before baking.
- Bake 45 minutes or until knife inserted comes out clean.

Banana Almond Fool

(Serves 8)

2 lemons	1 pint whipping cream
2 oranges	2 oz. castor sugar
8 ripe bananas (6 large)	*decoration:*
2 oz. ground almonds	2 oz. blanched almonds
2 oz. blanched almonds	4 tbsp. demerara sugar

- Finely grate orange and lemon rinds only taking the top zest.
- Squeeze out the lemon and orange juice from fruit.
- Mash 4 bananas and add most of the fruit juice. Add ground almonds and half of the zest. Blend well.
- Chop blanched almonds. Whip the cream until it just holds shape. Blend with banana mixture and castor sugar.
- Put into individual heat resistant serving dishes and chill well.

Topping:

- Slice remaining bananas, dip in remaining fruit juice and zest and spoon over Fool.
- Halve the almonds, sprinkle over the bananas and add the demerara sugar.
- Brown under grill. Chill until ready to serve.

Lacy Fingers

(Yields 24 cookies, Oven 375°)

½ cup flour
½ cup finely chopped walnuts
¼ cup corn syrup

¼ cup shortening
⅓ cup packed brown sugar

- Combine flour and walnuts.
- In a medium saucepan bring corn syrup, shortening and sugar to boiling point over medium heat, stirring constantly. Remove from heat and gradually stir in the flour and nut mixture.
- Onto a lightly greased baking sheet, drop dough by teaspoonful, about 3" apart.
- Bake for 5 minutes; cool 2 - 3 minutes before removing from baking sheet. (Do not allow cookies to cool completely before removing.) It is best to bake about 8 cookies at a time.
- While cookies are still warm roll them into cylindrical shapes.

Preparation Note: Easiest to roll around a pencil or wooden doweling. If cookies harden before shaping, return to the oven for a moment to soften.

Trick or Treats

Peanut Raisin Clusters

(Yields 1½ dozen)

½ lb. semi-sweet chocolate
⅔ cup sweetened condensed milk

1 cup whole peanuts
1 cup raisins

- Melt chocolate in top of double boiler; remove from heat.
- Add sweetened condensed milk, peanuts and raisins; mix well.
- Drop by teaspoonsful onto waxed paper and chill several hours before serving.

Serving Suggestion: These can be individually wrapped in saran or waxed paper and stored in the fridge until ready to be given as treats.

Caramel Popcorn Balls

(Yields 15)

5 tbsp. butter
1 cup brown sugar
½ cup light corn syrup

⅔ cup sweetened condensed milk
½ tsp. vanilla
5 quarts popped corn.

- In a saucepan combine butter, brown sugar and corn syrup. Stir well and bring to a boil over medium heat.
- Stir in condensed milk, stirring constantly until mixture reaches soft ball stage (234° on candy thermometer). Stir in vanilla.
- Pour syrup over popcorn and toss well until popcorn is coated. Butter hands and shape coated popcorn into balls about 3½" in diameter.
- Wrap in saran.

Crunchy Caramel Apples
(Yields 6 medium apples)

50 caramels (14 oz. package)   chopped walnuts
2 tbsp. water   6 wooden skewers
6 medium apples

- Melt caramels with 2 tbsp. water in top of double boiler. Stir frequently and continue cooking until mixture is smooth.
- Stick wooden skewers three quarters of the way into core of apples.
- Dip apples in caramel syrup and turn until bottom half of apples are completely coated. (If syrup is too stiff, add a few more drops of water).
- At once, roll bottoms of coated apples in chopped walnuts.
- Set apples on cookie sheet covered with waxed paper. Chill until caramel coating is firm.

Candy Apples
(Yields 8 apples)

8 wooden skewers   1⅓ cups light corn syrup
8 crisp medium apples   2 cups water
4 cups sugar   dash of salt

- Stick wooden skewers three quarters of the way into core of apples.
- Butter sides of heavy saucepan and combine sugar, corn syrup, water and salt. Bring to a boil stirring constantly. Continue cooking without stirring until mixture reaches hard crack stage (350° on candy thermometer). Remove from heat.
- Turn each apple in syrup, twisting apple to coat evenly letting excess syrup drip off into pan.
- Place apples on buttered cookie sheet and chill until firm.

No-Bake Peanut Butter Balls
(Yields 2 dozen)

1 cup peanut butter   1 cup Rice Krispies
1 tbsp. butter   ½ tsp. vanilla
1 cup icing sugar

- Blend all ingredients together with your hands. Shape into small balls.

Preparation Note: Children will love to help you make this recipe.

Nut Brittle

2 tbsp. butter   ⅔ cup sugar
2 tbsp. corn syrup   2 cups of your favourite nuts

- In a heavy pan, combine butter, syrup and sugar. Heat until sugar has dissolved.
- Add nuts. Cook and stir over medium heat until mixture is golden brown (10 to 15 minutes).
- Pour onto foil lined baking sheet. (Be sure to use foil, not waxed paper).
- Cool and break up into small pieces.

Dark Christmas Cake

(Yields 24 lbs. cake, Oven 325°)

5 lbs. seedless raisins
2 lbs. mixed peel
1 lb. orange peel
1 lb. candied pineapple
1 lb. glazed red cherries
1 lb. glazed green cherries
1 24 oz. bottle grape juice
1 lb. whole almonds, blanched
1 lb. pecan halves
½ lb. walnut pieces
2½ tbsp. rosewater

1 lb. butter
2½ cups packed brown sugar
3½ cups flour
1 tbsp. cinnamon
1 tbsp. nutmeg
1 tbsp. cloves
1 tbsp. allspice
1 dozen eggs
2 tbsp. melted bitter chocolate
1 24 oz. jar grape jelly

- Twenty four hours ahead:
  (a) soak raisins, peel, and cherries in grape juice
  (b) soak nuts in rosewater.
- Cream butter and brown sugar.
- Coat fruit in 1½ cups of the flour.
- Add spices to remaining 2 cups of flour and sift to blend.
- Alternately add 3 eggs and blended flour until all eggs and flour are used and batter is completely mixed.
- Melt chocolate and add to batter.
- Mix jelly into batter.
- Place floured fruit, nuts and batter in a large bowl and mix. This takes a lot of strength, so ask all the family to help. (A stir of the Christmas cake affords each a year of good health and happiness.)
- Grease pans and line with parchment paper or a double layer of greased waxed paper. You need pans that have removable bottoms. (Recipe will fill 7 pans measuring 6½" in diameter and 4" in height.) Fill pans to within an inch from top.
- Place a coffee can or other container of water in oven to ensure moist heat while cooking cakes. Bake 325° for 2 hours and then reduce heat to 250° and continue baking approximately 3 more hours. Test by inserting a skewer or long piece of straw into centre of cakes. If it comes out clean, cake is done.
- Leave cakes in pans until completely cooled.
- Remove from pans. Store wrapped in double layer of foil and place in cupboard.

Preparation Note: (1) These cakes are best made 2 months ahead and will stay fresh for a year or two if tightly sealed in foil and stored in a cool place. Can also be frozen.
(2) Rosewater can be purchased from the pharmacist at most drug stores.

'Tis the Season

Drop In For A Drink
Fabulous Finger Foods
Christmas Cookies
You'll Brunch
Wrap-Up Casserole
Trim The Tree
Gingerbread House

Chapter Two: 'Tis The Season

'Tis The Season

Those few weeks prior to Christmas can be relaxed and enjoyable if you take the time to prepare ahead. The following chapter has been designed with this in mind; so you can entertain your friends in your home and take the time to wish them the very best of the season. We are presenting some unusual liquid refreshments along with a variety of tasty finger foods, most of which may be prepared ahead of time. We are also offering a selection of Christmas cookies which is sure to please both family and friends.

And since the whole mood of the season can be so delightful, we would like to suggest that you give your Yuletide get-togethers a theme which reflects the spirit of Christmas. What about a Progressive Present Wrapping Party, or a Tree Trim-In with lots of popcorn and ju-jubes for stringing? Don't forget an early morning Tree Cutting Get-Together with warming drinks and a delicious brunch to follow.

But what would the drop-in season be like without displaying the traditional Gingerbread House in your home—a joy for both young and old? Try your hand at creating our Gingerbread House; even little fingers can be helpful, and the result truly may be a source of pride at this joyous time of year.

Compliments of the Season!

_____"Drop In For A Drink"_____

Mayor's Centennial Punch
(Yields 80 servings)

6 oranges
6 lemons
2 cups water
4 cups sugar
¼ tsp. salt
½ cup light corn syrup or maple syrup

2 cups lemon juice
64 oz. orange juice
60 oz. soda water
2 bottles sauterne or dry white wine
2 bottles white champagne

- Spiral peel oranges and lemons and place peels and fruit in saucepan.
- Add water, sugar, salt and corn syrup. Heat to boiling and simmer 15 minutes, stirring as required. Cover and let cool.
- Strain liquid into punch bowl.
- Squeeze fruit into liquid and, reserve peels. Add juices and mix.
- Cool with ice, stirring occasionally.
- Just before serving, add soda, wine and champagne. Add peels for colour.

Cinnamon Cider
(Serves 4)

32 oz. real apple cider
5 oz. white or light rum

cinnamon
4 cinnamon sticks

- Combine cider and rum in a large saucepan and place over medium heat.
- Sprinkle a powdery film of cinnamon on top of cider rum mixture.
- Stirring frequently, bring mixture to bubbling, but do not boil.
- Divide into 4 mugs and float a cinnamon stick in each.

Rosey Shake
(Serves 4)

1 pint strawberry ice cream
1½ cups fresh or frozen strawberries

1 cup rosé wine
½ cup milk

- Blend all ingredients and serve at once.

Merry Berry
(Serves 1)

1½ oz. vodka
1½ oz. cranberry juice

½ oz. collins mix

- Mix all ingredients in old-fashioned glass.
- Fill with ice. Serve.

Rye Flip
(Serves 1)

1 egg
½ tsp. sugar

1½ oz. rye
nutmeg

- Place all ingredients in a shaker and shake with ice.
- Strain into a small wine glass and sprinkle with nutmeg.

Traditional Christmas Eggnog
(Yields 12 cups)

6 eggs separated
¼ tsp. salt
⅔ cup sugar
¾ cup light rum

1 tsp. vanilla
2 cups whipping cream
2½ cups milk
nutmeg

- Beat egg whites and salt until stiff peaks form. Set aside.
- Beat egg yolks until light. Gradually add sugar and continue beating until thick and lemon coloured. Slowly stir in rum and vanilla.
- Whip cream until soft peaks form. Fold whipped cream and egg whites into yolk mixture.
- Gently stir in milk.
- Serve well chilled with nutmeg on top.

Anonymous Eggnog
(Yields 2 quarts)

⅓ cup sugar
3 egg yolks
¼ tsp. salt
4 cups milk, scalded
1 tsp. vanilla

3 egg whites
3 tbsp. sugar
½ cup whipping cream
nutmeg

- In top of double boiler, beat ⅓ cup sugar into egg yolks.
- Add salt and slowly stir in milk.
- Cook, stirring constantly until mixture coats the spoon.
- Add vanilla and remove from heat. Cool.
- Beat egg whites until foamy.
- Gradually add 3 tbsp. sugar, beating until soft peaks form.
- Add egg whites to custard and mix thoroughly. Chill a few hours.
- Top with an island of whipped cream and sprinkle with nutmeg.

Eggnog Alexander
(Yields 3 quarts)

⅓ cup creme de cacao
⅔ cup brandy

2 quarts eggnog
nutmeg

- Stir creme de cacao and brandy into eggnog.
- Sprinkle with nutmeg.

Fabulous Finger Foods

Shrimp Mousse
(Yields 4 cups)

1 10½oz. can tomato soup
8 oz. cream cheese
1 pkg. gelatin
1 medium onion, grated

½ cup celery chopped fine
½ cup mayonnaise
2 7oz. cans baby shrimp, drained
salt

- In a double boiler combine soup, cheese and gelatin. Heat until cheese has melted.
- Add remaining ingredients. Mix well.
- Pour mixture into a greased 4 cup mold.
- Refrigerate at least 4 hours.

Preparation Note: Place greased mold in freezer while preparing mousse. This helps later in unmolding mousse neatly and easily. This recipe can be made and kept up to two days before serving.
Serving Suggestion: Serve with assorted crackers.

Pâté De Foie Sans Fuss!
(Yields 4 cups)

1 10½oz. can consommé
salt and pepper
¼ tsp. garlic powder

¼ tsp. Worcestershire sauce
1 envelope gelatin
2 3oz. cans pâté de foie

- Heat consommé in a medium saucepan. Add salt and pepper to taste, garlic and Worcestershire. Bring to a boil.
- Empty gelatin into a cup. Add a few drops cold water to soften. Add softened gelatin to consommé.
- Empty cans of pâté de foie into a 4 cup mold and break up with a fork. Pour a small amount of consommé into pâté and mix slightly.
- Pour remaining consommé into mold (do not mix).
- Refrigerate approximately 4 hours.
- Turn out of mold to serve.
Serving Suggestion: Serve with assorted crackers. Can be made a day ahead and covered.

Salmon Cheese Ball

8 oz. cream cheese, softened
1 1lb. can of salmon, drained
1 tbsp. lemon juice

1 tsp. horseradish
¼ tsp. salt
parsley flakes

- Mix cream cheese and salmon together.
- Add lemon juice, horseradish and salt.
- Chill until you can form a ball.
- Roll in parsley.
Serving Suggestion: Serve with an assortment of crackers.

Favourite Freezer Mushroom Rolls

(Yields 8 dozen, Oven 400°)

4 10 oz. cans mushrooms, drained
⅔ cup butter
2 tsp. lemon juice
4 green onions, chopped
2 tbsp. butter

6 tbsp. flour
1 pint half and half
salt and pepper
2 loaves sliced white bread, crusts removed

- Finely chop mushrooms.
- Melt butter in pan and add lemon juice. Add mushrooms and cook 5 minutes over medium heat. Sprinkle green onions over mixture. Remove from heat.
- In another pan, melt 2 tbsp. butter and stir in flour. Gradually blend in cream. Add seasonings.
- Add mushroom mixture to cream mixture and cook over medium heat, stirring constantly until very thick, about 8 minutes.
- Remove mixture to heat proof bowl. Cover and refrigerate until cool.
- Meanwhile, with a rolling pin, roll 48 bread slices very thin.
- When mixture is well chilled, spread each slice with approximately 1½ tbsp. of mixture. Roll up jelly roll fashion.
- Pack rolls in plastic container, wrap container in foil and freeze.
- To serve, defrost and bake in a preheated oven, seams down, for 8 minutes or until golden brown. Or, place frozen rolls in preheated 350° oven and bake 15 to 20 minutes. Brush with melted butter before baking if desired. Cut rolls in half. Serve warm.

Shrimp Vegetable Dip

4 oz. cream cheese, softened
3-4 tbsp. mayonnaise
1 7oz. can small shrimp, drained

1 green onion, chopped
salt and pepper
paprika

- Whip cream cheese and mayonnaise.
- Stir in shrimp.
- Add green onions, salt and pepper to taste.
- Place in serving dish and sprinkle with paprika.

Serving Suggestion: Serve with a tray of mixed raw vegetables.

Cheese Ball

8 oz. cream cheese, softened
3 oz. chive flavoured cream cheese,
   softened
½ lb cheddar cheese, grated
2 tsp. Worcestershire sauce

½ tsp. garlic salt
¼ cup milk
⅓ cup chopped pecans

- Combine cream cheese, cheddar, Worcestershire, garlic and salt.
- Add milk, a little at a time, and blend in. Chill.
- Shape into a ball.
- Roll in chopped pecans. Wrap in Saran and refrigerate.

Serving Suggestion: Serve with a selection of crackers.

Carefree Corned Beef Pâté

1 12oz. can corned beef
8 oz. cream cheese, softened and cubed
1 6oz. can mushrooms, drained

¼ cup milk
1 envelope onion soup mix
2 sprigs parsley

- Break beef into chunks and put half into blender. Blend until well chopped. Remove to a bowl. Repeat with remaining beef.
- Put remaining ingredients into blender and blend until smooth. Combine cheese mixture and meat. Mix well.
- Smooth into attractive bowl or several small pots. Chill well.

Serving Suggestion: Serve with assorted crackers or dry bread. This can be prepared a day ahead and kept covered.

Crabmeat Appetizers
(Yields 20)

10 slices bacon, cut in half
½ cup fine dry bread crumbs
5 oz. can crabmeat, flaked
⅛ tsp. parsley
1 egg, beaten

2 tbsp. tomato sauce
¼ tsp. salt
⅛ tsp. pepper
1 tbsp. lemon juice
¼ tsp. Worcestershire sauce

- Partially cook bacon but do not brown. Drain on paper and set aside.
- Mix bread crumbs and crabmeat in bowl.
- Add parsley, egg, tomato sauce, salt, pepper, lemon and Worcestershire sauce and mix.
- Form into small balls and wrap half a slice of bacon around each and secure with a toothpick.
- Broil 10 to 15 minutes, turning frequently.

Scramble Mix
(Yield: 9 cups, Oven 250°)

¼ cup butter
¼ cup margarine
1 tbsp. seasoned salt
2 cups Shreddies

2 cups Cheerios
10 oz. Chinese noodles
2 cups mixed nuts
2 cups thin pretzel sticks

- In a shallow roasting pan melt butter and blend in seasonings.
- Stir in dry ingredients.
- Bake approximately 1 hour, stirring with a wooden spoon every 15 minutes.

Practical Pepper Cheese

8 oz. cream cheese, softened   pinch garlic powder
salt   ¼ tsp. paprika
fresh ground pepper to taste   ¼ tsp. dill weed

- Cream cheese and add spices. Mix well.
- Smooth cheese into small attractive pots. Chill.

Serving Suggestion: Serve with assorted crackers.

Antipasto

(Yields 15 pints)

2 large green peppers   2 15oz. bottles ketchup
4 large carrots (4 cups)   1 15oz. bottle hot ketchup
2 cans pitted black olives   1 cup red wine
1 16oz. jar broken green olives   2 5½oz. cans tomato paste
2 12oz. jars pickled onions   1 tbsp. oregano
2 4oz. cans pimiento   2 14oz. cans artichokes
1 48oz. jar sweet mixed pickles   2 10oz. cans mushroom pieces
1 large cauliflower   2 cans anchovies, chopped
8 oz. olive oil   3 7oz. cans solid tuna
5 cloves garlic, crushed

- Chop green peppers, cut carrots into julienne strips.
- Chop ripe olives, green olives, pickled onions, pimiento, sweet pickle and set aside.
- Break cauliflower into bite sized pieces.
- Put 2 oz. of olive oil into frying pan and add 2 cloves garlic; add cauliflower and sauté. Remove from heat and set aside.
- In large pot add remaining olive oil and sauté the remaining 3 cloves of garlic, add ketchup, wine, tomato paste and oregano.
- Add chopped vegetables, pickles, olives, artichokes, pimiento, cauliflower and mushrooms.
- Simmer for 10 minutes, stirring frequently.
- Add anchovies and tuna to mixture and bring to a boil, stirring constantly to prevent sticking.
- Place mixture immediately into hot sterilized jars, or place in containers for freezing.

Serving Suggestion: Serve on crackers.

Christmas Cookies

Pecan Gems
(Yields 3 dozen, Oven 275°)

¾ cup butter
5 tbsp. brown sugar
2 tbsp. ice water
1 tsp. vanilla

1 tsp. almond extract
2 cups sifted flour
1 cup chopped pecans
¼ cup icing sugar

- Cream butter and sugar.
- Add ice water, vanilla and almond extract. Gradually mix in flour and nuts.
- Pinch small pieces of dough and roll lengthwise (like fingers).
- Bake 40 minutes on ungreased cookie sheet.
- Dust icing sugar over warm cookies.

Christmas Cake Cookies
(Yields 5 dozen, Oven 375°)

¾ lb. dates
¼ lb. candied cherries
¼ lb. candied pineapple
¼ lb. shelled almonds
¼ lb. shelled Brazil nuts or
    chopped pecans
1¼ cups sifted flour

½ tsp. baking soda
½ tsp. salt
½ tsp. cinnamon
½ cup butter
¾ cup sugar
1 egg

- Chop dates and cherries and sliver pineapple. Coarsely chop almonds and toast in a 350° oven for 3 minutes, or until golden. Chop Brazil nuts.
- Sift flour, baking soda, salt and cinnamon together.
- Cream butter. Add sugar gradually and mix until smooth.
- Beat in egg, then stir in sifted ingredients and nuts.
- Drop cookie batter from teaspoon onto greased cookie sheet. Bake 10 minutes.

Grandma's Scotch Shortbread
(Yields 2 dozen, Oven 300°)

4 cups flour
8 tbsp. rice flour

1 cup fruit sugar
1 lb. butter, softened

- Grease a 15¾″ x 10½″ pan with a thin coat of butter and sprinkle with rice flour.
- Sift dry ingredients onto work area, add butter and knead well to a putty-like consistency.
- Press into pan and prick deeply with a fork. Mark into squares with a knife.
- Bake at 300° for 20 minutes, bake at 250° for 10 additional minutes, and then at 200° for 10 minutes longer. (It is a pale brown in colour when done.)

Peanut Butter Balls
(Yields 3 dozen)

1 cup peanut butter	1 tsp. vanilla
1 cup icing sugar	1 tbsp. butter
1 cup walnuts, chopped	4 semi-sweet chocolate squares
1 cup dates, finely chopped	1 square of parafin wax

- Combine first 6 ingredients and roll into small balls. Place in refrigerator until set.
- In top part of double boiler melt chocolate squares and parafin wax.
- Dip balls in chocolate mixture and place on waxed paper in refrigerator to cool.

Christmas Wreaths
(Yields 4 dozen, Oven 400°)

½ cup honey	¼ tsp. salt
½ cup molasses	½ tsp. baking soda
¾ cup brown sugar	1 egg, beaten
1 tbsp. lemon juice	2½ cups flour
2 tsp. grated lemon peel	3″ cookie cutter, round
1 tsp. cinnamon	1″ cookie cutter, round
1 tsp. ginger	silver shots
1 tsp. nutmeg	mixed candied fruits
¼ tsp. allspice	

- Heat honey and molasses in a saucepan until bubbly. Cool to lukewarm.
- In mixing bowl, combine sugar, lemon juice, peel, spices, salt, baking soda and egg.
- Add honey-molasses mixture and mix well.
- Add flour gradually and blend until smooth. Divide into 4 mounds.
- Cover tightly and refrigerate over night.
- Working with one mound of dough at a time, on a floured surface, roll out to ¼″ thickness.
- Dip 3″ round cookie cutter in flour and cut dough. Place round cuttings on greased cookie sheet and cut out centre of each with 1″ round cutter.
- Chop up candied fruits and press into cookies with silver shots.
- Bake for 10 to 12 minutes or until golden brown.
- Cool on rack.
- Store in airtight containers at least one week before serving.

Festive Fingerprints
(Yields 4½ dozen, Oven 325°)

2 cups flour
¾ cup icing sugar
1 cup finely chopped walnuts

1 cup butter, softened
1 tsp. vanilla
raspberry jam

- Combine flour, sugar and ½ cup of chopped nuts in a mixing bowl.
- Cut in butter with a fork until well mixed.
- Add vanilla and work dough with hands until smooth.
- Shape into 1½" balls and roll each in remaining nuts.
- On greased cookie sheet, place balls about 1" apart. Press middle finger into each and fill with sufficient jam.
- Bake for 15 to 18 minutes or until golden brown. Cool on rack.

Brandy Bobbles
(Yields 4½ dozen)

2 cups finely crushed vanilla wafers
2 cups icing sugar
2 cups chopped pecans
4 tbsp. cocoa

4 tbsp. corn syrup
½ cup brandy
½ cup sugar

- Stir together wafer crumbs, icing sugar, pecans and cocoa.
- Add corn syrup, brandy, and mix well.
- With wet hands, shape into 1 to 1½" balls.
- Roll each ball in sugar.
- Store in airtight container.

Shortbread Cookies
(Yields 3 dozen, Oven 325°)

1 cup butter
½ cup icing sugar

½ cup cornstarch
2 cups flour

- Cream butter until creamy but not oily.
- Sift dry ingredients. Add to butter a little at a time, working in with a spoon until dough no longer absorbs dry ingredients.
- Turn mixture onto floured board and knead until mixture cracks slightly. Dough may be put through a cookie press, rolled into balls and pressed, or patted gently to ⅓" thickness and cut with fancy cutters.
- Bake for 20 minutes on ungreased cookie sheet.

Kris Kringle Cookies
(Yields 3 dozen, Oven 375°)

½ cup butter	2 eggs beaten
¼ cup shortening	2¼ cups flour
1 tsp. vanilla	1½ tsp. baking powder
1 cup sugar	½ tsp. salt

- Cream butter and shortening. Add in vanilla, sugar and eggs. Blend well.
- Gradually add dry ingredients and blend.
- Roll onto a floured surface and cut with various cookie cutters.
- Bake 8 to 10 minutes on a greased cookie sheet.

Preparation Note: These are fun cookies for children to make and are nice Christmas decorations. To decorate brush with egg white while cookie is still hot and sprinkle with various coloured sugars and cake decorations.

You'll Brunch
(for 6)

Iced Grapefruit Juice
Cheese Crêpes
Sour Cream and Spinach Salad
Apricot Fluff
(Tangerines)

Iced Grapefruit Juice
(Serves 6)

1 12oz. can frozen grapefruit juice concentrate	18 ice cubes mint, fresh or dried
½ can water	

- Place all ingredients except mint in blender and blend until ice becomes slushy.
- Divide into 6 old-fashioned glasses. Top each with a pinch of mint. Serve at once.

Serving Suggestion: Nice with an ounce of rum or vodka added.

Cheese Crêpes
(Serves 6, Oven 400°)

1 recipe Crêpes (below)   1 recipe Cream Sauce (below)
1 recipe Cheese Filling (below)

Crêpes

1¼ cups flour   1½ cups milk
pinch salt   2 tbsp. butter, melted
3 eggs, beaten

- Mix all ingredients until all lumps are gone.
- Place a small amount of batter in oiled 5″ frying pan. Tip to spread batter. Cook over medium heat until lightly browned. Remove with spatula. Repeat. Stack to cool.

Cheese Filling

7 tbsp. butter   4 egg yolks
9 tbsp. flour   pepper
2 cups + 2 tbsp. milk, warmed   nutmeg
4 oz. grated Swiss or Gruyère cheese
1½ oz. grated Sapaago cheese (Romano or
    Parmesan may be substituted for
    different flavour)

- Melt butter in a saucepan and stir in flour.
- Cook roux a few minutes and add the warmed milk gradually, beating all the while with a wire whisk.
- When sauce is perfectly smooth and thick, stir in the grated cheeses.
- Remove sauce from heat and beat in egg yolks.
- Season with black pepper and nutmeg.
- Set ½ cup aside to use in Cream Sauce.
- Oil a square baking pan and spread the sauce over the bottom. Chill for several hours or until stiff enough to cut.
- Prepare crêpes as directed.
- Cut the stiff cheese sauce into about 20 narrow oblongs, each about 1″ wide and 3″ long.
- Wrap a crêpe around each oblong, tucking under the sides as you wrap.
- Arrange these crêpes in a lightly buttered baking dish.

Cream Sauce

2 tbsp. butter   ½ tsp. salt
2 tbsp. flour   dash pepper
1 cup milk   ½ cup Cheese Filling (above)
dash nutmeg   Parmesan cheese

- Melt butter in saucepan. Stir in flour. Continue cooking for 3 minutes without browning.

- Add milk, nutmeg, salt and pepper, and stir. Cook until thickened.
- Add reserved ½ cup of Cheese Filling.
- Pour Cream Sauce over filled crêpes and dust with Parmesan cheese.
- Cook in oven approximately 20 minutes. Crêpes should be soft inside and bubbling hot.

Preparation Note: Filled crêpes can be made ahead, covered and refrigerated until ready to cook.

Sour Cream and Spinach Salad
(Serves 6)

1 lb. spinach
½ cup chopped Spanish onions
¼ lb. fresh mushrooms

1 recipe Dressing (below)
¼ lb. crisply fried bacon
chopped parsley (garnish)

- Prepare Dressing (below).
- Toss spinach, onions and mushrooms with dressing. Sprinkle with bacon and garnish with parsley.

Dressing

½ pint sour cream
1 tbsp. lemon juice

½-1 tsp. hot mustard

- Blend all ingredients.

Apricot Fluff
(Yields 1 quart)

1 cup dried apricots
1¼ cups water
⅔ cup sugar

2 cups whipping cream
½ cup chopped almonds
1 tsp. grated orange rind

- Simmer apricots in water about 20 minutes or until tender.
- Add sugar and cook 5 minutes longer.
- Whirl fruit in blender. Cool.
- Whip cream, fold in apricot pulp, almonds and orange rind.
- Spoon into a 4 cup mold. Freeze until firm.
- To serve, unmold on a chilled platter and slice.

Wrap-Up Casserole
(for 8)
**Herbed Consommé
Crab and Artichoke Casserole
Great Brown Bread
Marinated Green Beans and Onions
Spiced Oranges
(Christmas Cookies)**

Herbed Consommé
(Serves 8-10)

2 tbsp. butter
2 celery stalks, minced
2 medium carrots, minced
1 medium onion, minced
4 10½oz. cans beef consommé

3 cups water
2 tsp. chervil
1 tsp. dill weed
1 tbsp. parsley to garnish

- Melt butter in saucepan and add celery, carrots and onions. Simmer until tender (approximately 15 minutes).
- Stir in undiluted consommé, water, chervil and dill. Heat to boiling.
- Serve garnished with parsley.

Preparation Note: This may be prepared ahead and stored in the refrigerator.

Crab and Artichoke Casserole
(Serves 10, Oven 350°)

¼ cup butter
3 tbsp. minced onion
½ cup flour
1 qt. table cream
½ cup Madeira
salt and pepper

2 tbsp. lemon juice
4 cups fresh or canned crabmeat
3 9oz. pkgs. frozen artichoke hearts, cooked
2½ cups cooked, drained macaroni shells
2 cups grated Gruyère or Swiss cheese
paprika

- Melt butter in a large heavy pan.
- Add onion and sauté until golden.
- Stir in flour, cooking over low heat until flour is pale yellow.
- Remove from heat and add cream, stirring vigorously.
- Return to moderate heat and stir until sauce comes to a boil.
- Remove from heat and add Madeira.
- Return to low heat and season with salt and pepper.
- Pour lemon juice over crabmeat and toss lightly.
- Combine crab, artichoke hearts, macaroni and sauce together in a six quart buttered casserole.

- Cover with cheese and dust with paprika.
- Bake 25 to 30 minutes or until heated through.

Preparation Note: If preparing a day ahead, complete first 10 steps. Refrigerate. Bring to room temperature and place in preheated oven for 25 to 30 minutes.

Great Brown Bread
(Serves 8, Oven 325°)

1½ cup bran flakes
1 cup milk
2 cups flour
⅔ cup sugar
2 tsp. baking powder
¾ tsp. salt

¼ tsp. baking soda
1 egg, beaten
¼ cup molasses
¼ cup shortening, melted and slightly
    cooled

- Soften bran flakes in milk.
- Sift dry ingredients.
- Stir egg, molasses and shortening into softened bran flakes.
- Add flour and stir to moisten.
- Pour mixture into greased 9″ x 5″ x 3″ pan.
- Bake for 1 hour. Cool in pan for 10 minutes before removing to cooling rack.

Marinated Green Beans and Onions
(Serves 8)

4 large carrots, sliced
2 lbs. cut green beans

2 medium onions, thinly sliced
1 recipe Dressing (below)

- Cook carrots and beans until tender
- Separate onion slices into strips.
- Combine ingredients in salad bowl.
- Cover with Dressing and toss. Place in refrigerator and allow to marinate for several hours. Toss frequently.

Dressing

1 cup wine vinegar
½ cup oil

1 tsp. sugar
½ tsp. dry mustard

- Blend all ingredients.

Spiced Oranges
(Serves 8)

1½ cups water
½ cup sugar
peel of 4 oranges
6 whole cloves

5 cinnamon sticks
8 oranges, peeled and sectioned
3 tbsp. lemon juice

- In saucepan combine water and sugar, peel and spices. Bring to a boil and cook 10 minutes.
- Remove peel from pot and discard. Add orange sections to pan and cook 2 minutes.
- Remove pan from heat, add lemon juice and cool. Chill for 12 hours.
- Remove to serving bowl and serve with Christmas cookies (See pages 30 to 33).

Trim The Tree
(for 8)
Lasagna
Mediterranean Salad
Garlic Bread
Cherries Jubilee

Lasagna
(Serves 8, Oven 350°)

2 lbs. ground beef
1 cup chopped onion
1 garlic clove, crushed
1 12oz. can tomatoes
1 15oz. can tomato sauce
1½ tbsp. parsley flakes
1½ tbsp. sugar
1 tsp. salt
1 tsp. basil

1 tsp. oregano
1 lb. cottage cheese
½ cup Parmesan cheese
1 tbsp. parsley
1 tsp. salt
8 oz. lasagna noodles, cooked and drained
¾ lb. Mozzarella cheese, shredded or sliced

- Brown ground beef, onion and garlic in large frying pan.
- Add tomatoes, tomato sauce, 1½ tbsp. parsley flakes, sugar, 1 tsp. salt, basil and oregano. Simmer 1 hour, uncovered.
- Mix cottage cheese, Parmesan cheese, 1 tsp. parsley and 1 tsp. salt.
- In a large pan (13½″ x 9″ x 2″) layer cooked noodles, sauce and cottage cheese mixture until all is used, finishing with sauce on top.
- Sprinkle Mozzarella over top. Bake for 45 to 50 minutes.

Preparation Note: This is a good dish to make ahead and freeze. Thaw and bake for about 45 minutes.

Mediterranean Salad
(Serves 6-8)

1 large head romaine lettuce
3 tomatoes, cut in wedges
½ cucumber, sliced
¼ cup chopped green onions
½ red onion, sliced in rings

6 radishes, sliced
1 stalk celery, diced
½ cup black olives, sliced
¼ cup crumbled feta cheese
1 recipe Dressing (below)

- Toss ingredients together and chill.
- Dress just before serving.

Dressing

6 tbsp. olive oil
2 tbsp. wine vinegar
1 tsp. minced garlic

1 tsp. oregano
salt and pepper

- Combine ingredients and blend.
- Pour over salad when ready to serve. Serve at once.

Cherries Jubilee
(Serves 8)

2 cups pitted sweet cherries (canned or preserved)
¼ cup slightly warmed brandy

3 tbsp. Kirsch liqueur
vanilla ice cream

- Heat cherries in chafing dish.
- Add brandy and ignite.
- When flames have gone out, add Kirsch.
- Serve hot over ice cream.

Serving Suggestion: Spectacular display when prepared at table.

Gingerbread House
(10″ x 12″ house. Oven 375°)

Components:
Graph paper or construction paper to make pattern for house. (See Pattern, page 42).
Lots of colourful candies, candy canes and stick candies.
1 recipe Gingerbread (see next page)
1 recipe Snow Frosting (see next page)
Lots of patience!

Construction of House:
- Cut out pattern pieces from paper.
- Prepare Gingerbread as directed.
- On a floured surface, roll out dough to ⅛″ thickness.
- Cut out each pattern piece from dough.
- Bake each piece separately on a greased cookie sheet for 6-10 minutes. (Windows will distort slightly while cooking). While Gingerbread is still warm, place pattern on each piece and trim areas of Gingerbread which have expanded more than ⅛″ beyond pattern.
- Allow to cool before removing from cookie sheet.
- Prepare Snow Frosting as directed below.
- Generously frost edges of front and back and wall pieces of house. Put in place and tie with a string until dry.
- Frost gables of house and apply roof pieces. Fill in peak and any other open spaces with icing. Hold in place.
- Pipe frosting on house where candies will be used for decorating. Frosting will hold candies in place.

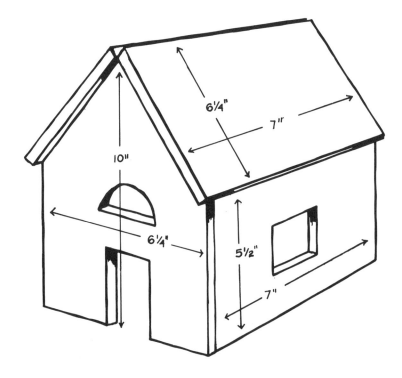

Gingerbread

1 cup shortening
1 cup sugar
½ tsp. salt
1 egg
1 cup molasses
2 tbsp. vinegar

4 cups flour, sifted
1½ tsp. baking soda
1 tbsp. ginger
1 tsp. cinnamon
1 tsp. ground cloves

- Thoroughly cream shortening, sugar and salt together.
- Stir in egg, molasses and vinegar. Beat well.
- Sift together all dry ingredients and stir into molasses mixture.
- Chill for 3 hours.

Snow Frosting
(Yields 4 cups)

6 egg whites (room temperature)
2 lb. icing sugar
1 tsp. cream of tartar
2-3 drops of blue food colouring

- Place egg whites, icing sugar and cream of tartar in a bowl and beat at medium speed, 7 to 10 minutes. Mixture should be very stiff.
- Blend in blue food colouring to make icing nice and white.
- Cover bowl with a damp cloth until ready to use.
- Place in a decorating bag to apply to house.

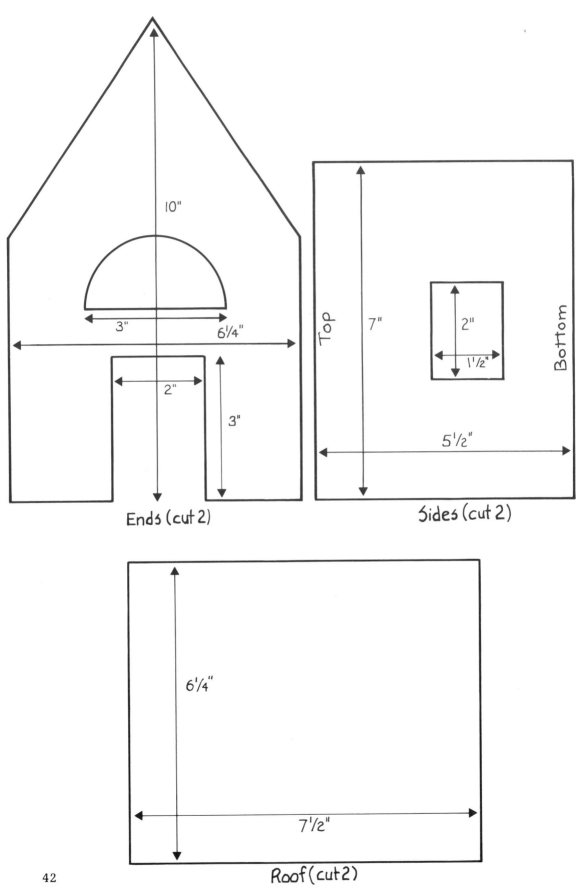

10"

3"

6¼"

2"

3"

Ends (cut 2)

Top

7"

2"

1½"

5½"

Bottom

Sides (cut 2)

6¼"

7½"

Roof (cut 2)

42

Christmas

Réveillon
Brunch Amongst The Wrappings
Traditional Christmas Dinner
Boxing Day Slow Down

Chapter Three: Christmas
Réveillon
Brunch Amongst The Wrappings
Traditional Christmas Dinner
Boxing Day Slow Down

Christmas

Christmas has always been the most sacred of holidays. It is a season filled with traditions meant to be shared with friends and family, for as the carols remind us, it is a time for goodwill toward men.

Now that we have enjoyed warming up and preparing for Christmas—the tree is decorated, the gingerbread house is in place, and the stockings are about to be hung—this chapter presents our thoughts and suggestions for the three very special days of Christmas: Christmas Eve, Christmas Day, and Boxing Day.

On Christmas Eve, the French people in many Georgian Bay communities carry on a tradition called Réveillon. When translated, this means midnight supper. At midnight, family members would attend mass together and return home to a hearty dinner. After the meal, gifts would be opened under the Christmas tree. This is a wonderful tradition to keep alive even if it is held at an earlier hour or date. Réveillon just might provide the perfect setting for your special Christmas celebration with friends.

When the turkey is brought to the family table on Christmas Day, the setting is truly complete. It seems that the turkey has always been the bird of celebration, but many years ago it was the goose which served this purpose. In the old days, the goose could be raised around the barnyard comfortably feeding itself off the pasture or orchard, while the turkey had to be penned in and required more care and attention to its fattening. In this chapter we are presenting a truly traditional Christmas menu with the goose as the highlight of the dinner. Merry Christmas.

Boxing Day has always provided us with the time to slow down after Christmas. It is also a day to try out the new skis, skates and sleighs. A family outing might be to Lafontaine where one finds the most beautiful cross-country ski trails. The Boxing Day dinner should be easy so as not to interfere with the day's activities, whatever they may be.

It should also utilize yesterday's leftovers. Try our menu for this and the other important days of the Christmas holiday. Joined with them are our compliments of this wonderful season.

Réveillon
(for 8)
Mushroom and Green Pepper Salad
Dinner Rolls
Tourtière
Last Minute Chili Sauce
Cranberry Apple Pork
Oven Fried Potatoes
Parmesan Brussels Sprouts
Eggnog Custard Pudding

Mushroom and Green Pepper Salad
(Serves 8)

1 lb. mushrooms, sliced
juice of half a lemon

2 large green peppers, slivered

* Place mushrooms and green pepper in bowl.
* Toss with Dressing. Serve chilled.

Oil and Vinegar Dressing

1 clove garlic, crushed
¼ tsp. salt
1 tsp. pepper

9 tbsp. olive oil
3 tbsp. wine vinegar

* Blend all ingredients.

Dinner Rolls
See Basics, page 209

Tourtière
(Yields 1 pie, Oven 450°)

There are several versions of Tourtière either using all ground pork or a combination of pork and rabbit, or beef. We usually make pies well in advance and freeze them. They're nice to have on hand for last minute company.

Allow approximately 2 lbs. meat for a 9 inch pie.

Recipe for one 9″ double crust pastry
    (See Basics, page 212)
1½ lbs. lean ground pork
½ lb. lean ground beef
1 cup water
1 medium sized onion, chopped

1 small bay leaf
2 celery tops, chopped
pinch ground cloves
salt and pepper to taste
½ cup fine bread crumbs

- Place meat in skillet and add water.
- Add onion, bay leaf, celery tops and seasoning.
- Bring to a boil and simmer approximately 45 minutes, until bulk of liquid has evaporated. Let cool.
- Stir in bread crumbs and place in pie shell.
- To bake, place in 450° oven for 15 minutes.
- Reduce oven temperature to 350° and continue cooking for 30 minutes or until brown.

Preparation Note: If placed in oven while frozen, allow additional 15 minutes to bake.

Last Minute Chili Sauce
(Yields 1½ cups)

2 16oz. cans tomatoes	pinch cayenne pepper
¼ cup mixed pickling spice	½ cup mild vinegar
1 onion chopped	⅛ cup sugar
½ tsp. salt	3 tbsp. green pepper, chopped

- Drain tomatoes.
- Place pickling spices in a cheese cloth bag.
- Combine all ingredients and simmer 1½ hours.
- Remove from heat and bottle. Store in refrigerator.

Cranberry Apple Pork
(Serves 8, Oven 350°)

3 lb. loin end pork roast, bone removed	1 recipe Filling (below)
1 cup dry white wine	

Filling

¼ lb. fresh cranberries	1 tbsp. sugar
1 medium apple pared and sliced	¼ cup water

- Place cranberries, apples, sugar and water in a saucepan.
- Bring to a boil; cover and boil 3-4 minutes.
- Remove from heat and let cool.
- Mash mixture with a fork.
- Place cranberry Filling into bone cavity of roast.
- Secure opening with poultry skewers and kitchen twine. Tie roast in 2 or 3 places so it will hold its shape while cooking.
- Rub a little salt and pepper into fat side of roast.
- Pour wine over roast and place in preheated oven for 2½-3 hours, basting roast frequently.

Oven Fried Potatoes
(Serves 8, Oven 350°)

½ cup butter
½ tsp. salt
1 tsp. pepper

6 cups thinly sliced potatoes
2 medium onions, sliced

- Over low heat melt butter and add salt and pepper.
- Layer potatoes and onions in a baking dish.
- Pour melted butter over potatoes and toss.
- Place in oven and bake 1½ hours tossing occasionally.

Parmesan Brussels Sprouts
(Serves 8, Oven 350°)

1½ lb. cooked brussels sprouts
¼ cup Parmesan cheese

2 tbsp. butter

- Butter a shallow baking dish and sprinkle with Parmesan cheese.
- Add sprouts, sprinkle with more cheese and drizzle with melted butter.
- Bake for 20 minutes.

Eggnog Custard Pudding
(Serves 8, Oven 350°)

3 cups milk
3 tbsp. butter
3 cups cake crumbs (Butter sponge or
    White cake) (See Basics, Page 208)
4 eggs
½ tsp. salt

4 tbsp. sugar
1 tsp. vanilla
1 cup whipping cream, whipped
3 tbsp. rum
nutmeg

- Scald milk.
- Add butter and cake crumbs to scalded milk.
- Beat eggs, salt and sugar.
- Add scalded milk gradually to eggs, stirring constantly.
- Add vanilla.
- Turn mixture into a buttered 9″ ring mold; set mold in a pan and add hot water to a depth of 1″.
- Bake 35-40 minutes, or until an inserted knife comes out clean.
- Place in refrigerator.
- To serve, loosen custard around edge of mold and invert onto serving plate.
- Fill centre with whipped cream flavoured with rum.
- Dust cream with nutmeg.

Brunch Amongst The Wrappings
(for 8)
Fresh Fruit Salad
Arnold's Benedict
Cinnamon-Sour Cream Coffee Cake

Fresh Fruit Salad
(Serves 8)

2 apples
2 pears
2 oranges
3 bananas

½ lb. seedless grapes
maraschino cherries (optional)
1 large melon, balled
1 cup orange juice

- Cut apples and pears into small chunks.
- Divide oranges into sections and half again.
- Slice bananas.
- Wash and pull stems from grapes.
- Slice maraschino cherries in half.
- Shape melon balls.
- Mix fruit together in a bowl with orange juice and chill.

Serving Suggestion: For extra flavour, mix in ¼ cup Grand Marnier.

Arnold's Benedict
(Serves 8)

1½ cups mayonnaise
½ cup sour cream
2 tbsp. lemon juice
4 tsp. prepared mustard

4 English muffins, split and toasted
8 slices Canadian bacon, cooked
8 poached eggs
parsley for garnish

- Combine mayonnaise, sour cream, lemon juice and mustard in a saucepan; mix well over low heat, stirring constantly until thoroughly heated.
- On each muffin half, place one slice of bacon, one egg and cover with ⅛ of the sauce.
- Garnish with parsley.

Preparation Note: Canadian bacon is often referred to as Peameal Bacon.

Cinnamon-Sour Cream Coffee Cake
(Serves 8, Oven 350°)

1 cup butter
1½ cups sugar
2 eggs beaten
1 cup sour cream
1 tsp. vanilla

2 cups flour
1½ tsp. baking powder
½ tsp. baking soda
½ tsp. salt
1 recipe Topping (below)

Topping

2 tsp. cinnamon mixed with 4 tbsp. sugar

- Cream butter and sugar.
- Add eggs and mix well.
- Blend in sour cream and vanilla.
- In another bowl, blend flour, baking powder, soda and salt.
- Add flour mixture to cream mixture.
- Pour half of batter into a 9″ x 9″ ungreased pan and sprinkle with half of the Topping. Repeat.
- Bake 45 minutes.

MENU

Traditional Christmas Dinner
(for 8)
Roast Goose With Chestnut Stuffing
Broiled Orange Slices
Cranberry Cream Salad
Holiday Brussels Sprouts
Gourmet Onions
Creamy Mashed Potatoes
Mincemeat Meringues

Roast Goose With Chestnut Stuffing
(Serves 8, Oven 450°)

12-14 lb. goose   1 recipe Chestnut Stuffing (see next page)

- Clean and fill cavities with Chestnut Stuffing.
- Prick goose several times on legs and breasts.
- Place goose on a rack in an uncovered pan and place in hot oven.
- Reduce the heat at once to 350°.
- Allow 20 minutes per pound cooking time.
- Skim fat as it accumulates.

Chestnut Stuffing

½ cup butter
1 cup chopped onion
1 cup chopped celery
½ tsp. each oregano, sage, thyme, rosemary
2 lbs. fresh or canned chestnuts

½ cup water with 2 chicken bouillon cubes
2 lbs. dried bread, diced in cubes
3 eggs slightly beaten

- Melt butter in skillet and sauté onions and celery until soft.
- Add herbs, chestnuts, and water with bouillon cubes.
- Place bread in bowl and toss with eggs and chestnut mixture.

Broiled Orange Slices
(Serves 8)

5 oranges
4 tbsp. butter

3 tbsp. brown sugar
1 tsp. curry powder

- Cut oranges into ¾″ slices and place on baking sheet.
- Dot each slice with butter, sprinkle with brown sugar and dust lightly with curry.
- Broil and serve as garnish around goose.

Cranberry Cream Salad
(Serves 8)

1 small pkg. cherry flavoured gelatin
1 cup hot water
1 14oz. can cranberries

½ cup chopped walnuts
1 cup finely diced celery
1½ cups sour cream

- Dissolve jello in hot water. Chill till partially set.
- Add cranberries and stir into gelatin with walnuts and celery.
- Fold in sour cream.
- Pour into 6 cup mold; chill until firm.

Holiday Brussels Sprouts
(Serves 8)

3 lbs. brussels sprouts (10 cups)
¼ cup butter

¼ cup dry fine bread crumbs
2 tbsp. snipped parsley

- Cook sprouts and drain.
- Melt butter in skillet.
- Add crumbs and parsley.
- Spoon mixture over sprouts and toss lightly.

Gourmet Onions
(Serves 8)

16 small cooking onions, peeled
4 tbsp. butter
½ tsp. sugar

salt and pepper
¼ cup sherry
½ cup grated cheddar cheese

- Boil onions until tender.
- Melt butter, add sugar, salt and pepper to taste, and sherry.
- Add onions and heat quickly, stirring constantly.
- Turn into serving dish and sprinkle with grated cheese.

Creamy Mashed Potatoes
(Serves 8)

12 medium potatoes
1 cup sour cream

salt and pepper

- Boil potatoes and mash.
- Add sour cream, salt and pepper and whip well.

Mincemeat Meringues
(Serves 8-12, Oven 275°)

Meringue Shells (12 3″ meringues)

4 egg whites, room temperature
1 tsp. vanilla
¼ tsp. cream of tartar

dash of salt
1 cup sugar

Filling

1 pint rich vanilla ice cream

1 lb. prepared mince meat

- Beat egg whites, vanilla, cream of tartar and salt, until frothy.
- Gradually add sugar and beat until very stiff peaks form.
- Cover cookie sheet with ungreased paper (parchment or brown). Draw 12 3″ circles, spread each with about ⅓ cup of meringue. Shape with back of spoon to make shells.
- Bake in a very slow oven for 1 hour. Turn off heat; let dry in oven (door closed 1½ hours). Store meringues tightly covered until ready to use. Can be made several days ahead and frozen.
- To serve, place 1 scoop of ice cream in meringue shells and cover with warm mincemeat. Serve immediately.

Preparation Note: For mincemeat recipe, See Celebration Bombe. Page 60

Boxing Day Slow Down
(for 6)
Quick Turkey Paella
Pear Cranberry Salad
Herbed Rolls
Brazil Nut Coffee Cake

Quick Turkey Paella
(Serves 6, Oven 350°)

1 14oz. can tomatoes	1 tsp. garlic
2¼ cups tomato juice	1 cup uncooked rice
¼ cup oil	3 cups diced turkey
¼ cup chopped onion	¼ cup sliced stuffed green olives
¼ cup chopped green pepper	1 can button mushrooms
1 tsp. salt	Parmesan cheese

- In a large saucepan combine first 7 ingredients.
- Stir in rice, cover and bring to a boil.
- Add turkey, olives and mushrooms and turn into a 3 quart casserole.
- Bake uncovered for 45 minutes or until rice is tender; stir occasionally.
- Sprinkle with grated Parmesan before serving.

Pear Cranberry Salad
(Serves 6)

6 tbsp. cream cheese, softened	lettuce
½ cup chopped walnuts	6 tbsp. prepared cranberry sauce
6 canned pear halves	

- Combine cream cheese with chopped walnuts.
- Arrange lettuce on plates and place a pear half on each.
- Place 1 tbsp. cream cheese mixture on pear halves.
- Top with 1 tbsp. cranberry sauce.

Herbed Rolls
(Serves 6, Oven 350°)

12 baked dinner rolls (See Basics,
    page 209)
¼ cup butter, melted

½ tsp. each tarragon, sweet basil, thyme,
    sage, onion salt

- Thaw rolls, place in oven dish. Brush with melted butter.
- Combine herbs and sprinkle over rolls.
- Cover with foil and heat 10 minutes.

Brazil Nut Coffee Cake
(Serves 6, Oven 400°)

Topping

½ cup brown sugar
2 tbsp. tea biscuit mix (See Basics,
    page 211)

3 tbsp. butter, melted
½ cup chopped Brazil nuts

Batter

2 cups tea biscuit mix (See Basics,
    page 211)
1 tbsp. sugar

1 egg
¾ cup milk

- Combine ingredients for Topping and line bottom of pan with mixture.
- Mix batter ingredients; carefully pour over Topping.
- Bake for 20 to 25 minutes.
- Serve warm.

New Years

New Year's Eve Progressive Party
Just Four Hours Of Good Eating
Neptune's New Year
New Year's Buffet for 20
Crowning The Day

Chapter Four: New Year's

New Year's Eve Progressive Party
Just Four Hours Of Good Eating
Neptune's New Year
New Year's Buffet for 20
Crowning The Day

New Year's

There are many ways to bring in the new year. Some people prefer to sit by the fire and quietly toast a bright new year, while others like to have lots of friends and neighbours to share in the celebration at a big country dance.

In the Midland area, some of our friends have coupled their New Year's festivities with the beauty of a crisp and snowy winter's night. One small group usually starts the evening with torchlight cross-country skiing along the beautiful trails just outside of town. Then they warm up together over a very special midnight supper. One year it was suckling pig. Another year they flew in fresh lobster. Yet another year they enjoyed their own home-made Chinese food. Another group of our friends takes part in a neighbourhood progressive dinner party.

A progressive dinner party allows all to share in the entertaining, lessening the individual work load. The joint effort makes for a relaxed and delightful eve of celebration. Simply map out your course from house to house in the neighborhood, agree on a menu and assign each participant a course of the menu. Walk or ski from home to home wherever possible, enjoying an appetizer here, and then a hot bowl of soup there, a delicious helping of casserole at Jean's place, and a tasty dessert at Mary's. The exercise and fresh air between courses is a nice respite and heightens the appetite for the next course. A progressive dinner party is always an enjoyable get-together, and if you want to try it, we have designed an ideal menu in this chapter devoted to New Years.

New Years might also be that time of year when you choose to invite in a crowd of friends. Don't think that lots of people means lots of work when it comes time to feed them. If you plan a buffet carefully and choose those recipes which may be prepared ahead, you will definitely cut your work load in half. In this chapter we have planned a Buffet for 20 which will give you some delicious ideas for this all important occasion.

The family element is also very much in evidence at New Years, and in some homes a large family dinner is prepared for New Year's day. Our very special "Crowning the Day" menu provides the perfect ingredients for this feast.

Whatever you plan for New Years, make sure you mix the good cheer, warm wishes and high hopes with great food, and it will be a celebration to remember for many years to come.

Easy Cheesy Bread; Avocado, Orange and Blue Cheese Salad, page 60.

New Year's Eve Progressive Party
(for 12)

Stop #1 Cocktails	—"Martannies"
Hor D'Oeuvres	—Blue Cheese Puffs
	—Cocktail Sausages with Honey-Chili Dip
Stop #2 Appetizer	—Potato Soup
Stop #3 Entrée	—Beef and Artichoke Mélange
	—Easy Cheesy Bread
	—Avocado, Orange and Blue Cheese Salad
Stop #4 Dessert	—Celebration Bombe
	—Oriental Almond Cookies
Stop #5 Coffee	—Irish Coffee

"Martannies"
(Serves 12 2oz. drinks)

8 oz. dry vermouth   16 oz. vodka

- Mix ingredients well, put in an unbreakable container and place in the freezer for 4 to 5 hours.
- Serve in chilled glasses.

Preparation Note: Chill glasses by placing them in the freezer for several hours.

Blue Cheese Puffs
(Yields 40 puffs, Oven 400°)

1 pkg. refrigerator biscuits   1 4 oz. pkg. blue cheese, crumbled
¼ cup butter

- Cut each biscuit into quarters and arrange on 9" x 9" shallow pan or casserole.
- Melt butter and cheese in double boiler.
- Drizzle cheese mixture over biscuit pieces, being sure to coat them.
- Bake 10 to 15 minutes or until golden brown. Serve hot.

Cocktail Sausages With Honey-Chili Dip
(Serves 12)

5 dozen cocktail weiners
1 cup chili sauce
½ cup honey

1 tsp. curry powder (or to taste)
½ cup vegetable oil

- Heat cocktail weiners according to directions. Do not allow to split.
- Combine and stir chili sauce, honey, curry powder and vegetable oil in a medium sauce pan over medium heat until just bubbly.

Serving Suggestion: To serve, arrange sausages on a platter with dip in centre. Have toothpicks available.

Potato Soup
(Serves 12)

⅓ cup butter
2 medium onions, finely chopped
¼ cup celery leaves, finely chopped
6 medium potatoes, peeled and cubed small

6 cups boiling water
salt and pepper to taste
6 cups scalded milk

- In a large saucepan, melt butter over medium heat and sauté onions until light brown.
- Add remaining ingredients, except milk, and reduce heat. Cook covered 15 minutes or until potatoes are tender.
- Add scalded milk and reheat to boiling point. Remove from heat and serve immediately.

Preparation Note: This soup can be prepared and cooked ahead of time. Reheat before serving.

Beef and Artichoke Mélange
(Serves 12)

2 cups flour
salt and pepper
6 lbs. sirloin, cut in 2″ cubes
¼ cup oil
2 cloves garlic, crushed
5 8oz. cans tomato sauce

3 cups dry red wine
3 beef bouillon cubes
3 10½oz. cans small onions
3 pkg. frozen artichokes or 4 12oz. cans
3 10½oz. cans mushrooms, drained

- Combine flour, salt and pepper. Coat meat with flour mixture.
- In a large Dutch oven, heat oil over medium heat and brown garlic, then remove garlic.
- Brown meat in oil.
- Add tomato sauce, wine and beef bouillon cubes. Stir well. Continue cooking over medium heat for 30 minutes or until meat is tender.
- Add remaining ingredients and heat until warmed through.

Easy Cheesy Bread
(Serves 12, Oven 350°)

2 loaves frozen, uncooked bread   Parmesan cheese
¾ cup butter, melted

- Refrigerate bread and allow to thaw in package overnight.
- Slice each loaf into 12 slices.
- Dip each slice in butter and roll in Parmesan cheese.
- Place slices upright in a bundt pan.
- Allow bread to rise to top of pan (approximately 1½ to 2 hours).
- Bake bread for 30 minutes or until browned.

Avocado, Orange and Blue Cheese Salad
(Serves 12)

2 heads romaine lettuce   8 oz. blue cheese, crumbled
5 large oranges   1 recipe Lemon Dressing (below)
2 large, firm ripe avocados

- Arrange romaine in salad bowl.
- Pare and section oranges; refrigerate lettuce and oranges.
- Just before serving, peel, pit and slice avocados. Arrange avocados, oranges, and crumbled blue cheese over romaine.
- Drizzle Lemon Dressing over salad, toss gently.

Lemon Dressing:

(Yields ¾ cup)

¼ cup fresh lemon juice   ¼ tsp. sugar
½ tsp. salt   ¼ tsp. dry mustard
⅛ tsp. pepper   ½ cup vegetable oil

- Place lemon juice, salt, pepper, sugar and dry mustard in blender.
- Add oil in a slow stream until thick and creamy. Refrigerate.
- Shake well before using.

Celebration Bombe
(Serves 12)

2 pints black cherry ice cream, slightly   2 pints pistachio or spumone ice cream,
   softened   slightly softened
2 pints vanilla ice cream slightly   1 recipe Mincemeat Sauce (see next page)
   softened

- Several days ahead, assemble bombe in a 12 cup bundt pan, mold or bowl. Using the back of a spoon, press black cherry ice cream into pan, smoothing it firmly onto the sides and bottom of pan.
- Repeat process with vanilla and pistachio ice creams.
- Wrap tightly and place in freezer.

Mincemeat Sauce

1 16oz. jar of mincemeat
¼ cup dark corn syrup

¼ cup dark rum

- Place mincemeat and corn syrup in saucepan and bring to a boil for one minute. Add water to thin slightly, if necessary.
- Cool and stir in rum (sauce should be thick, but not runny). Serve warm.

To Serve:
- Loosen edges of bombe and quickly dip mold into warm water to the top of the pan. Dry.
- Invert bombe onto a chilled platter.
- Cut bombe into slices and top with Sauce.

Oriental Almond Cookies
(Yields 3-4 dozen, Oven 325°)

2¾ cups flour
1 cup sugar
½ tsp. soda
½ tsp. salt
1 cup butter

1 egg, slightly beaten
1 tsp. almond extract
⅓ cup whole almonds

- Sift flour, sugar, soda and salt together.
- Cut in butter until mixture resembles corn meal.
- Add egg and almond extract. Mix well.
- Shape dough into 1″ balls and place 2″ apart on ungreased cookie sheet. Press down to flatten slightly.
- Top each cookie with an almond.
- Bake for 15 to 18 minutes. Cool on racks.

Irish Coffee
(Yields 12 mugs)

12 oz. or jiggers Irish Whisky
12 tsp. sugar

12 cups strong coffee
chilled whipped cream

- Pre-warm mugs or goblets.
- In a large pot, heat but do not boil whisky and sugar.
- Place an equal amount of warmed whisky in each mug.
- Fill mugs to within 1″ of top with hot coffee. Stir until sugar is dissolved.
- Float a thick layer of whipped cream on top of liquid. Serve immediately.

Just Four Hours Of Good Eating!
(for 8)
Bloody Marys
Petites Quiches
Creamy Horseradish Ham Roll
Broiled Grapefruit
Madeira Consommé
Beef Bayfield
Broccoli in Cream
Romaine Lettuce With Curry Dressing
Peach Crêpes Flambées
Arnie's Armies

Bloody Marys
(Serves 8)

48 oz. tomato juice

4 dashes tabasco

6 dashes Worcestershire sauce

2 tsp. celery salt

2 tsp. sugar

4 tsp. lemon juice

2 lemon wedges

¼ cup coarse salt

8 oz. vodka

8 celery stalks

- Blend first 6 ingredients. Adjust seasoning to suit your own taste.
- Refrigerate until ready to serve.
- To serve, use highball glasses. Take lemon wedge and run it over the rim of the glass. Roll the moistened rim of glass in a dish of coarse salt. Place an ounce of vodka in glass and fill with tomato juice mixture. Use celery stick as a swizzle stick.

Petites Quiches
(Serves 24)

1 recipe Pastry (below)

1 recipe Filling (see next page)

Pastry

½ tsp. salt

½ cup grated cheddar cheese

1½ cups flour

⅓ cup cold butter

¼ cup cold lard or shortening

4 tbsp. ice water

- Stir salt and grated cheese into flour.
- Cut in butter and lard.
- Sprinkle with water and gather dough together into a ball. Refrigerate ½ hour.
- Roll out into a thin circle and cut out rounds with a 2½" cookie cutter. Re-roll extra dough and cut out more circles (makes 24).
- Fit into tart or muffin tins. Prick well and refrigerate at least ½ hour.
- Bake shells 5 minutes at 425°.

Filling

1 onion, finely chopped	1 cup Swiss cheese, grated
2 tbsp. butter	½ tsp. salt
½ lb. mushrooms, finely chopped	⅛ tsp. pepper
2 eggs	1 tsp. tarragon
¾ cup sour cream	⅛ tsp. nutmeg
	2 tbsp. chopped parsley

- Cook onions in butter until tender and add mushrooms. Cook until mixture is completely dry.
- Beat eggs with sour cream and stir in cheese.
- Add salt and pepper, tarragon and nutmeg.
- Place a little Filling in bottom of each tart and pour some of sour cream-egg mixture on top.
- Sprinkle each filled tart with parsley.
- Bake in preheated oven at 350° for 15 to 20 minutes until puffed and golden. Serve warm.

Creamy Horseradish Ham Roll
(Serves 8)

2 8 oz. pkg. cream cheese, softened	1 tsp. salt
4 tbsp. prepared horseradish	1 tsp. pepper
4 tbsp. mayonnaise	12 ham slices, approx. 4½″ x 6½″
2 tsp. Worcestershire sauce	

- Combine first 6 ingredients and mix well.
- Spread cream cheese mixture on ham slices and roll up jelly roll fashion. Refrigerate.
- When ready to serve, slice each roll in roughly ¾″ slices. Arrange in a single layer on a platter.

Broiled Grapefruit
(Serves 8)

4 large grapefruit	8 tsp. butter
8 tbsp. sherry	8 maraschino cherries
8 tsp. brown sugar	

- Cut each grapefruit in half and section.
- Place 1 tbsp. of sherry on each serving and allow it to soak in.
- Sprinkle a teaspoon of brown sugar on each and top with a teaspoon of butter.
- Place 3″ under broiler for a few minutes (until bubbly).
- Top with a cherry and serve immediately.

Madeira Consommé
(Serves 8)

6 tbsp. cold water
3 egg whites
2 carrots, minced
3 tbsp. parsley, minced

1 leek or small onion, diced
4 cups Beef Stock, (see Basics, page 207)
salt and pepper to taste
½ cup Madeira

- Place water and egg whites in a saucepan and beat to a froth.
- Add carrots, parsley and leek.
- Pour in cold Beef Stock.
- Season with salt and pepper. Bring to a boil stirring constantly.
- Reduce heat and simmer for 10 minutes stirring frequently.
- Strain through a clean damp cloth.
- Place in clean saucepan and add Madeira. Heat.

Preparation Note: Egg whites are used to clarify the consommé.

Beef Bayfield
(Serves 8, Oven 425°)

4 lb. eye of round roast
1 recipe Marinade (below)
1 recipe Mushroom Filling (below)

1 recipe Pastry (see next page)
1 recipe Gravy (see next page)

Marinade

¾ cup Burgundy wine
¾ cup port

1 medium sized onion, quartered
3 bay leaves

Day Ahead:
- Combine Marinade ingredients.
- Place roast and Marinade in a heavy plastic bag. Refrigerate, turning bag occasionally to distribute Marinade.

Mushroom Filling

8 oz. fresh mushrooms, chopped
1 leek (white only), chopped
3 tbsp. butter
¼ cup fine dry bread crumbs

3 tbsp. Marinade
½ cup liver pâté or 1 4¾oz. can liverwurst
   spread

- In a fry pan, place mushrooms, leek and butter. Sauté until tender (approx. 6 minutes).
- Remove from heat, add bread crumbs, 3 tbsp. Marinade and liver pâté.
- Cover and chill at least one hour.

To Cook Meat:
- Remove meat from bag, reserving Marinade.
- Place meat on a rack in a shallow roasting pan. Roast meat to 130° on meat thermometer (50 to 60 minutes).
- Remove from oven and cool at least 20 minutes, reserving pan drippings.

Pastry

2 cups flour
½ tsp. salt
⅔ cup shortening

⅓ to ½ cup cold water
1 beaten egg

- In a mixing bowl, combine flour and salt.
- Cut in shortening until mixture resembles small peas.
- Gradually add cold water, a tablespoon at a time, tossing with fork until mixture is dampened and begins to form a ball.
- Shape into a ball and roll out on a lightly floured surface (14″ x 12″ rectangle).

To Assemble:
- Spread Mushroom Filling on Pastry to within 1″ on all sides.
- Place meat, top side down on centre of Pastry.
- Place hand under Pastry on one side of roast. Carefully smooth Pastry along side of roast.
- Repeat for other side. Pastry should overlap slightly. Trim excess Pastry. To seal, brush with beaten egg.
- Seal ends off.
- Place roast seam down on a lightly greased baking sheet.
- Brush with beaten egg.
- Bake 425° for 30 minutes or until Pastry is golden brown.

Gravy

½ cup Marinade
pan drippings

¾ cup water
3 tbsp. flour

- In a saucepan, combine ½ cup Marinade with pan drippings. Heat thoroughly.
- Place flour and water in a jar and shake well until all lumps are gone.
- Slowly add flour mixture to heated Marinade mixture, stirring constantly.
- Cook until thickened. Season with salt and pepper to taste.

Preparation Note: Time first stage of cooking meat to scheduled time of guests arrival. Remove meat from oven, place on a platter and cover with a lid. Have pastry ready, rolled out and spread with pâté and cover with a damp cloth. Enjoy cocktails with guests.

Preheat oven to 425° prior to using broiler. Have grapefruit ready to place under broiler. Soup can be ready to pour into serving dishes.

Place roast in pastry as directed and put in oven at stated temperature and allow to cook while you are eating the grapefruit and soup. The second stage of cooking only takes a half hour.

Broccoli In Cream
(Serves 8)

3 lbs. broccoli
4 quarts water
1 tsp. salt

1 tsp. sugar
1 tbsp. butter
1 recipe Cream Sauce (below)

- Wash broccoli and trim stems. Cut stalks about the size of your thumb.
- Add broccoli to boiling salted water and return to boiling for 2 to 3 minutes.
- Drain immediately and set on paper towelling to dry.
- Place on serving dish and top with Cream Sauce.

Cream Sauce

2 tbsp. butter
½ cup whipping cream

1 tbsp. lemon juice
salt and pepper to taste

- Heat butter in saucepan, add cream, lemon juice, salt and pepper, stirring with a wire whisk constantly. Do not bring to a boil.

Romaine Lettuce With Curry Dressing
(Serves 8)

2 heads romaine lettuce

1 recipe Curry Dressing (below)

- Core and clean lettuce.
- Place leaves on layers of paper towels, refrigerate.

Curry Dressing

2 tbsp. vinegar
1 tbsp. lemon juice
1-2 tsp. curry powder (or to taste)

1 tsp. sugar
½ cup cream
½ cup sour cream

- Combine ingredients and blend well.

To Serve:
Place lettuce on salad plates and top with Dressing.

Peach Crêpes Flambées
(Serves 8)

1 recipe Dessert Crêpe (next page)
1 28oz. can peach halves
1 tbsp. cornstarch

½ cup brandy or orange liqueur
1 cup whipping cream, whipped

- Prepare Dessert Crêpes.
- Drain peaches reserving liquid.
- Arrange folded crêpes and peach halves alternately in a chafing dish.
- Mix juice, cornstarch and ¼ cup of brandy or orange liqueur. Heat to dissolve cornstarch.
- Pour sauce over peaches and crêpes and heat thoroughly.
- Heat remaining brandy and ignite. Pour over crêpes. Serve when flames die.
- Top with whipped cream.

Dessert Crêpe

1¼ cups flour
2 tbsp. sugar
pinch of salt
3 eggs

1½ cups milk
2 tbsp. melted butter
½ tsp. lemon, rum, or brandy extract
(optional)

- Blend all ingredients. For best results, let batter stand 1 hour before using.
- Cook each crêpe.
- Fold crêpes in wedge fashion (fold in half and fold again). Set aside.

Arnie's Armies
(Yields 1 drink)

1¼ oz. cognac   1¼ oz. Grand Marnier liqueur

- Combine cognac and Grand Marnier in brandy snifter; stir gently.
- Serve at room temperature.

MENU

Neptune's New Year
(Serves 4)
Oysters in Cream Cheese
Clam Chowder
Avocado and Crabmeat Salad
Stuffed Trout
Sautéed Potatoes
Green Pepper Platters
Crème Brulée

Oysters in Cream Cheese
(Yields 1½ cups)

3 oz. can smoked oysters (or mussels)
2 tsp. lemon juice
8 oz. cream cheese, softened

2 tbsp. mayonnaise
pinch of pepper
3 dashes tabasco sauce

- Drain oysters and chop fine. Sprinkle with lemon juice.
- Cream the cheese. Beat in mayonnaise, pepper and tobasco until light and creamy. Stir in chopped oysters. Taste and adjust seasonings.
- Place covered in refrigerator until ready to serve.

Serving Suggestion: Nice served on a mild tasting cracker, or melba round.

Clam Chowder
(Serves 4)

2 slices bacon
1 cup onion, finely chopped
2 cups potatoes, pared and cubed
1 tsp. salt
dash pepper

1 cup water
2 10½oz. cans clams
2 cups half and half cream
3 tbsp. butter

- Chop bacon. Sauté in a large pot until almost crisp.
- Add onions and cook 5 minutes.
- Add cubed potatoes, salt, pepper and water. Cook uncovered for 15 minutes or until potatoes are done. Place in blender or food processor and blend until smooth.
- Drain clams, reserving liquid.
- Place potato mixture, clams, ½ clam liquid, cream and butter in a large pot. Mix well over medium heat. Serve hot.

Serving Suggestion: Nice served topped with a dash of Madeira.

Avocado and Crabmeat Salad
(Serves 4)

1 ripe avocado
2 tsp. onion, grated
1 tsp. fresh lemon juice
pinch salt
2 drops tabasco sauce
1 cup chili sauce

1 tsp. horseradish
pinch sugar
1 7oz. can crabmeat (drained and chilled)
lettuce leaves

- Slice avocado in half. Cover and refrigerate one half until serving time. Peel remaining half and mash.
- Add onion, lemon juice, salt and tabasco and mix well. Refrigerate.
- Mix chili sauce, horseradish and sugar. Cover and refrigerate.
- To serve, arrange lettuce leaves on individual plates. Cut and chop reserved avocado and mix with crabmeat. Place on lettuce.
- Place chili sauce mixture over crabmeat.
- Top with mashed avocado mixture.

Stuffed Trout
(Serves 4, Oven 350°)

4 whole trout
¼ tsp. salt
¼ tsp. white pepper
¼ tsp. tarragon

4 tbsp. butter
4 tbsp. vegetable oil
1 recipe Stuffing (see next page)

- Season trout with seasonings.
- Place butter and oil in heavy skillet. Fry fish until golden brown.
- Remove fish from pan and debone. (Cut off head, tail and fins. With a spoon gently separate the spine from the fish. If cooked enough, the bones come away easily. Make sure all bones have been removed.)

Stuffing

7 stalks celery
2 leeks or green onions
1 medium carrot
1 cup mushrooms
1 14oz. can artichokes

1 clove garlic, crushed
1 cup dry white wine
2 tbsp. butter
2 tbsp. flour
4 oz. whipping cream

- Finely chop vegetables and combine with wine in saucepan. Simmer 5 minutes.
- In separate saucepan, combine butter and flour, stirring constantly until golden brown.
- Whisk in cream and cook until smooth and thickened.
- Stir in vegetable mixture.
- Spread Stuffing inside each trout.
- Place in greased pan and bake 15 to 20 minutes.
- Serve with lemon wedges.

Preparation Note: Fish may be prepared early in the day, stuffed and set aside to be heated immediately before serving.

Green Pepper Platters
(Serves 4, Oven 350°)

2 medium green peppers
¼ cup chopped onion
2 tbsp. butter
1 medium tomato, chopped
⅓ cup lima beans, cooked

⅓ cup whole kernel corn
1 tbsp. butter
½ cup bread crumbs
1 tsp. dill weed

- Cut peppers in half, lengthwise. Remove membrane and seeds. Cook in boiling salted water for 5 minutes. Drain on paper towel and sprinkle insides lightly with salt.
- Sauté onion in 2 tbsp. butter. Add tomato, lima beans and corn. Mix well.
- Fill peppers with vegetable mixture and place in a baking dish.
- Melt 1 tbsp. butter. Add bread crumbs, dill weed, and mix together. Sprinkle over filled peppers.
- Bake for 30 minutes.

Sautéed Potatoes
(Serves 4)

4 potatoes, peeled
1 tsp. salt
1 tsp. sugar
1 tbsp. butter

2 tbsp. vegetable oil
2 tbsp. butter
parsley

- Quarter potatoes and round edges.
- Place in boiling water with salt, sugar and butter. Cover, heat and simmer until tender. Drain and place over heat to dry.
- Sauté in oil and butter.
- Sprinkle with parsley and serve.

Crème Brulée

(Serves 4)

3 eggs
1½ cups whipping cream

1 tbsp. butter
1 tbsp. sugar
1 cup brown sugar

- Beat eggs well and set aside.
- Heat cream in a double boiler. Add butter.
- Pour hot cream over eggs while beating constantly.
- Return to double boiler and stir in sugar. Heat until mixture thickens and custard coats spoon.
- Place in a greased baking dish or individual custard cups. Refrigerate at least 12 hours.
- Sift brown sugar over custard. (There should be approximately ¼" brown sugar on top of custard.)
- Place in a cold oven and turn the heat to 250°. Heat until sugar is caramelized. (It doesn't take long and needs watching.)

New Years Buffet
(for 20)

Champagne Punch
Escargot Pâté
Pineapple Bacon Cubes
Devilled Eggs

Veal Savory
Holiday Beef Balls
Baked Avocados
Marinated Buffet Salad
Tomato Aspic
Sweet Pepper Salad

Buttered Noodles Parmesan
Cheese Twists
Ambrosia
Cream Puffs

Champagne Punch
(Yields 2 qts., 20 Servings)

2 6oz. cans frozen concentrated orange
  juice
1 6oz. can frozen concentrated lemonade
6 cups cold water

1 qt. champagne
1 cup mixed fresh fruit (bananas, orange
  sections and strawberries)

- Mix orange juice, lemonade and water; chill.
- To serve, pour juice mixture into punch bowl. Add champagne and mix. Float fruit on top.

Escargot Pâté
(Serves 20)

1 cup butter
6 garlic cloves, crushed
2 tbsp. white wine
2 9oz. tins drained escargots

2 8oz. cream cheese
3 tbsp. chopped parsley
4 tsp. dill weed
6 green onions

- Melt butter with garlic and wine. Add escargots, cover and simmer 5 minutes, stirring occasionally.
- Cut cheese into 1″ cubes and combine with parsley, dill, and chopped onion in food processor or blender.
- Add escargot mixture to processor; add ground pepper and process 30 seconds.
- Remove pâté to serving crocks. Chill.
Serving Suggestion: Serve with cracker assortment.

Pineapple Bacon Cubes

1 lb. bacon slices, cut in half   2 16oz. can pineapple tidbits

- Wrap bacon around pineapple piece and secure with a tooth pick.
- Place on broiler rack and broil, turning until bacon is crisp. Serve hot.

Devilled Eggs

1 doz. eggs, hard boiled   ½ cup green relish
1 cup mayonnaise   ½ cup minced onion
2 tsp. prepared mustard   paprika garnish

- Halve eggs lengthwise and remove egg yolks. Mash and combine yolks with remaining ingredients.
- Refill egg whites.
- Sprinkle with paprika. Chill.

Veal Savory

(Serves 20, Oven 325°)

1 cup flour   5 whole cloves
3 tsp. salt   1 tsp. thyme
1 tsp. pepper   1 tsp. tarragon
5 lbs. veal cutlets (about 24 medium) 1 tsp. marjoram
¾ cup butter   1 cup white wine
1 large clove garlic   2 cups Chicken Broth (see Basics, page 207)
12 carrots, quartered   2 cups pork sausage cut in
4 cups thinly sliced onions (8 onions)   small pieces
3 bay leaves   3 tbsp. parsley

- Mix flour, salt and pepper. Dredge cutlets in seasoned flour.
- Melt butter in large skillet and use to brown cutlets and garlic.
- Place carrots, onions, bay leaves, spices, wine and broth in large roasting pan or casseroles.
- Add browned meat. Bake for 1½ hours.
- Meanwhile sauté sausages until done; add to veal just before serving. Garnish with parsley.

Holiday Beef Balls
(Makes 12 doz., Oven 350°)

5 lbs. ground beef
2 cups finely chopped onion
1½ cups soft bread crumbs
4 eggs
4 tbsp. paprika
¼ cup dill
2 tbsp. dry mustard

salt and pepper
½ cup butter
2 cups Beef Stock (see Basics, page 207)
2 6oz. tomato paste
⅛ cup Worcestershire sauce
2 cups sour cream

- Combine first 7 ingredients with salt and pepper to taste and mix well. Shape into small balls.
- Melt butter in large skillet(s) over medium heat. Add meatballs and brown evenly. Remove.
- Combine stock, tomato paste and Worcestershire sauce in saucepan and bring to boil over high heat.
- Remove from heat and stir in sour cream.
- Pour over meatballs and simmer 10 minutes.
- Transfer to serving dish(es).

Preparation Note: Meatballs may be frozen in their sauce and reheated over low heat on stove or in moderate oven (350°). Do not allow sauce to boil.

Baked Avocados
(Serves 20, Oven 300°)

½ cup lemon juice
1 cup water
10 ripe avocados, halved and pitted
½ cup butter
½ cup flour

3 cups milk
¾ tsp. salt
1 cup grated cheddar cheese
5 cups cubed ham
1 tbsp. chopped chives

- Pour lemon juice and water into shallow pan.
- Place avocado halves, with cut sides down, in juice.
- Melt butter in top of double boiler; blend in flour.
- Add milk and salt; cook and stir until mixture has thickened.
- Add cheese, ham and chives, blending well.
- Keep mixture hot over boiling water.
- Turn avocado halves cut sides up.
- Pour warm water into pan to about ½″ depth.
- Heat in slow oven for 10 to 15 minutes.
- Remove half shells to serving dish and fill with cheese-ham mixture. Serve at once.

Marinated Buffet Salad
(Serves 20)

1 recipe Marinade Dressing (below)
2 bunches broccoli, cut into bite-sized
    pieces
2 heads cauliflower, cut into small
    flowerets
2 pints cherry tomatoes
8 stalks celery, diced

8 carrots, sliced in small strips
12 green onions, chopped
2 10oz. cans whole mushrooms, drained
2 14oz. cans pitted black olives, drained
2 4oz. cans red pimiento, drained and
    chopped

- Prepare Marinade Dressing (below).
- Put all fresh vegetables and canned ingredients into a double plastic garbage bag.
- Add Dressing; shake bag a few times and tie top in a tight knot.
- Refrigerate bag and marinate for 24 hours, turning frequently.

Serving Suggestion: Drain vegetables thoroughly just before serving. Arrange salad in a large salad bowl.

Marinade Dressing

2½ cups vegetable oil
1½ cups red wine vinegar
1 tbsp. sugar
1 tbsp. dry mustard

2 tsp. garlic powder
2 tsp. onion powder
2 tsp. dill weed
salt and pepper

- Combine all ingredients and blend.

Tomato Aspic
(Serves 20)

2 tbsp. unflavoured gelatin
4 cups tomato juice
⅓ cup chopped onion
¼ cup chopped celery leaves
2 tbsp. brown sugar
1 tsp. salt

2 small bay leaves
4 whole cloves
3 tbsp. lemon juice
½-1 cup finely chopped celery
2 tbsp. chopped green pepper
lettuce

- Soften gelatin in 1 cup cold tomato juice.
- Combine 2 cups of tomato juice with next six ingredients.
- Simmer uncovered 5 minutes; strain.
- Dissolve softened gelatin in the hot tomato juice mixture. Add remaining tomato juice and the lemon juice. Chill until partially set.
- Stir in celery and green pepper.
- Pour mixture into a 5½ cup ring mold. Chill until firm, 5 to 6 hours or overnight.
- Unmold on chilled platter (on a bed of lettuce).

Serving Suggestion: This will make 20 small servings. Make two to allow for more generous servings.

Sweet Pepper Salad
(Serves 20)

8 green peppers
8 red peppers
⅔ cups white wine vinegar
4 tbsp. medium dry sherry
2 tbsp. Worcestershire sauce
⅔ cups olive oil

2 tsp. salt
½ tsp. pepper
4 tsp. sugar
2 tsp. paprika
20 pitted black olives
12 oz. cream cheese, cubed

- Halve peppers and remove white pith and seeds. Cut peppers in quarters. Blanch peppers for 3 minutes. Drain and dry. Cool.
- In large mixing bowl combine vinegar, sherry, Worcestershire sauce, oil, salt and pepper, sugar and paprika. Taste; add more seasonings if necessary.
- Put peppers in marinade; turn and mix until they are coated with dressing. Cover and marinate 24 hours in fridge.
- To serve, place the peppers in a shallow dish or bowl. Spoon a little marinade over them. Place olives and cheese over the top and serve.

Buttered Noodles Parmesan
(Serves 20)

3 pkgs. egg noodles (3 lbs.)
2 cups butter

1 cup grated Parmesan
salt and pepper

- Cook noodles according to package directions until "al dente." Drain well and place in serving dish.
- Melt butter over medium heat. Add to noodles and toss gently.
- Add Parmesan, salt and pepper. Serve warm.

Serving Suggestion: Serve in chafing dish or on warmer; best kept warm.

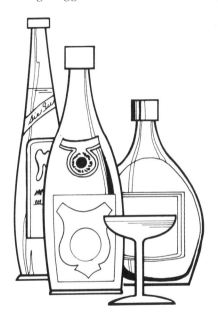

Cheese Twists
(Yields 48, Oven 375°)

2 pkgs. active dry yeast
5-5½ cups flour
2 cups milk
1½ cups cubed cheddar cheese
½ cup sugar

¼ cup butter
1 tbsp. salt
1 egg
½ cup butter, melted

- Activate yeast according to package directions.
- In large mixing bowl, combine 2 cups flour and yeast.
- In saucepan heat milk, cheese, sugar, butter and salt until just warm (115° to 120°) and butter and cheese are almost melted; stir constantly.
- Add to flour mixture; add egg.
- Beat at low speed for 1 to 2 minutes, scraping sides of bowl constantly.
- Beat 3 minutes at high speed, stirring in as much of the remaining 3½ cups flour as you can mix in with a spoon.
- Turn out onto lightly floured surface.
- Knead in enough of the remaining flour to make a soft dough; continue kneading until smooth and elastic (5 to 8 minutes).
- Shape into a ball. Place in lightly greased bowl, turning once to grease surface.
- Cover and let rise in warm place until double (about 1½ hours).
- Punch dough down; turn out onto lightly floured surface.
- Divide dough into four equal pieces; shape each into a ball. Cover and let rest 10 minutes.
- Roll each ball into a 12″ x 6″ rectangle. Cut crosswise into 6″ x 1″ strips.
- Tie each strip into a loose knot.
- Place 2″ to 3″ apart on greased baking sheet, cover and let rise until double in size (about 40 minutes).
- Brush with melted butter. Bake 10 to 12 minutes or until brown.

Ambrosia
(Serves 20)

8 cups pineapple chunks
pineapple juice
3 cups orange sections
6 ripe bananas
2 cups orange juice

5 cups seedless grapes
3 cups flaked coconut
whole maraschino cherries
1 7oz. bottle ginger ale

- Drain pineapple reserving syrup.
- Pare oranges with sharp knife; remove sections by cutting close to membrane.
- Peel and slice bananas and place in orange juice.
- Wash grapes and dry.
- In large bowls arrange alternate layers of oranges, bananas, pineapple and grapes. Sprinkle each layer with coconut, ending with a layer of coconut. Dot with maraschino cherries.
- Pour reserved pineapple juice over all. Chill thoroughly.
- At serving time add ginger ale. Serve.

Cream Puffs

(Yields 24 large or 72 small, Oven 400°)

2 cups water	½ tsp. salt
1 cup butter	2 cups flour
2 tsp. sugar	8 eggs
	1 recipe Strawberry Filling (below)
	1 recipe Vanilla Filling (below)
	1 recipe Chocolate Topping (below)

- Combine water, butter, sugar and salt in saucepan. Bring to a full boil.
- Add flour at once. Stir quickly with wooden spoon until mixture forms a thick and smooth ball (about 1 minute).
- Remove from heat and add eggs, beating well after each addition with an electric beater until paste is smooth and shiny.
- Drop by spoonfuls onto an ungreased sheet or press through pastry bag to make them fancy.
- Bake in hot oven for 30 to 40 minutes or until golden brown.

Strawberry Filling (Please note: this will fill half the Cream Puffs)

1 pint strawberries	2 tbsp. icing sugar
(fresh or frozen)	1 cup whipping cream

- Slice berries and add 1 tbsp. icing sugar. Chill.
- Beat cream until stiff, gradually adding the remaining tbsp. of sugar. Chill.
- Cut the tops off the puffs and remove any soft dough.
- Fold berries and cream together and then spoon into puffs. Replace the tops.
- Sprinkle extra icing sugar over the tops.

Note: You can use any fruit combination.

Vanilla Filling (Please note: this will fill half the Cream Puffs)

1¼ cups milk	⅓ cups flour
3 egg yolks	½ tbsp. vanilla
⅓ cup white sugar	1 tbsp. butter

- Heat milk until it begins to bubble.
- Beat yolks and sugar. Beat in flour and mix well, then gradually beat in the hot milk.
- Return mixture to saucepan and cook until mixture thickens. Stir continuously.
- When mixture is quite thick, remove from heat and add vanilla and butter. Chill several hours. To prevent a film forming on top of custard, cover the surface with Saran wrap.
- Fill a pastry bag with Vanilla Filling and squeeze into the puffs, or if you have made éclairs, make a small hole in the end of the éclair and press filling into the éclair. Replace top on the puff and drizzle with Chocolate Topping.

Chocolate Topping

½ square unsweetened chocolate	½ cup icing sugar
½ tbsp. butter	½ tsp. vanilla
1 tbsp. hot water	

- Melt butter and chocolate over low heat. Stir in sugar, hot water and vanilla until smooth.
- Drizzle over tops of puffs.

Crowning The Day
(For 12)
Shrimp Cocktail
Crown Pork Roast With Eggplant Stuffing
Royal Roast Potatoes
Finnish Carrots
Spinach Salad With Sauce Vinaigrette
Frozen Lemon Frost Supreme

Shrimp Cocktail
(Serves 12)

lettuce   1 recipe Seafood Sauce (below)
2 lbs. shrimp

- Line seafood cocktail glasses with lettuce. Hook 6 to 8 cooked and shelled shrimp over the edge of each dish. Place Seafood Sauce on bed of lettuce.

Seafood Sauce

¾ cup chili sauce   ¼ cup horseradish

- Blend chili sauce and horseradish well. Chill.

Crown Roast Of Pork
(Serves 12, Oven 350°)

Have the butcher roll you a crown of pork. The following recipe will feed 12 people easily but you can have him prepare a smaller crown for fewer people. Have him include the ground pork you need in the recipe.

Pork

crown of pork (16 to 24 ribs)   1 tsp. marjoram
1 tsp. salt   1 recipe Stuffing (below)
                                                spiced crabapples
                                                parsley

- Rub salt over pork. Press marjoram into pork.
- Prepare Stuffing (see next page)
- Fill cavity in crown with Stuffing. Protect Stuffing with a cover of foil and cover each rib bone with foil. Place on a metal rack in open roasting pan and cook 35 minutes per pound.

To Serve: Replace foil with coloured paper frills or a spiced crabapple on each rib bone. Garnish with parsley.

Stuffing

½ cup oil
3 cloves garlic
1 medium eggplant, cubed and unpeeled
½ cup flour
1 tsp. salt
½ tsp. pepper
2 tbsp. butter

2 onions, diced
1 lb. ground pork
1 cup bread crumbs
1 tbsp. fresh parsley, chopped
1 tsp. mixed herbs (thyme, marjoram)
½ tsp. salt
¼ tsp. pepper

- Heat oil in skillet. Sauté garlic until golden.
- Coat eggplant with flour, salt and pepper, and sauté in oil until brown. Remove and drain. Discard garlic.
- Add butter and diced onions and sauté. Add ground pork and brown. Remove excess fat and mix in eggplant, crumbs, parsley, mixed herbs, salt and pepper. Cool.

Royal Roast Potatoes
(Serves 12, Oven 350°)

14 medium potatoes
garlic powder

½ cup oil
paprika

- Peel potatoes and quarter. Place potatoes in casserole dish and add oil, turning potatoes until they are completely coated in oil.
- Sprinkle with garlic powder and paprika.
- Place in oven and bake 1 hour or until well browned and crispy. Serve hot.

Finnish Carrots
(Serves 12)

4 cups carrots, slivered
1 cup onions, chopped
¼ cup butter
2 tbsp. parsley, chopped

1½ tbsp. sugar
salt and pepper to taste
3 tbsp. flour
1½ cups milk

- Cook carrots until tender; don't over cook.
- Sauté onions in 1 tbsp. of butter, set aside.
- Place remaining butter in saucepan. Heat; add flour to make roux; add milk, beating with wire whisk. Add sugar, salt and pepper, parsley and cooked onions. Stir frequently, cooking for 5 minutes.
- Place cooked carrots in serving dish and mix well with sauce. Serve hot.

Spinach Salad With Sauce Vinaigrette
(Serves 12)

3 lbs. fresh spinach
4 hard boiled eggs, separated
½ cup crisp bacon bits

1 recipe Sauce Vinaigrette (below)
½ cup croutons

- Clean and dry spinach. Tear into bite-sized pieces and place in salad bowl.
- Press egg yolks through a fine sieve and chop egg whites.
- Toss eggs and bacon bits into salad.
- To serve, add dressing and toss. Top with croutons.

Sauce Vinaigrette

¼ cup white or red wine vinegar
salt and pepper

½ tsp. dry mustard
¾ cup olive or salad oil

- Place all ingredients in container and blend well.

Frozen Lemon Frost Supreme
(A Frozen Soufflé)
(Serves 12)

2 egg yolks
¼ cup sugar
1 tbsp. + 1 tsp. flour
1 cup milk, heated just below boiling
¼ tsp. vanilla

2 cups whipping cream
1 cup lemon juice
7 egg whites, room temperature
¼ tsp. cream of tartar
¼ tsp. salt
1 cup + 1 tbsp. sugar

- Place egg yolks in saucepan and beat with whisk until light and frothy.
- Gradually add sugar beating constantly until mixture is thick and lemon coloured.
- Add flour and beat until smooth.
- Add hot milk, a little at a time, beating until well blended.
- Place saucepan over medium heat and cook, stirring constantly with whisk, until mixture is thick and coats spoon (about 5 to 6 minutes).
- Pour mixture into a bowl and stir in vanilla. Cool slightly. (This mixture is often referred to as Crème Pattissière and can be made ahead and refrigerated several days. Bring to room temperature and whisk until loosened before using.)
- Cut strip of foil long enough to wrap around a 1½ quart soufflé dish. Fold in half lengthwise. Generously butter one side and sprinkle with sugar. Wrap around dish letting foil extend about 4″ above rim. Secure with string or tape.
- Whip cream in a large bowl until soft peaks form. Fold in cream mixture (Crème Pattissière) and lemon juice. Set aside.
- Whip egg whites in separate bowl until foamy. Add cream of tartar and salt, and continue beating until soft peaks form. Gradually add sugar, beating constantly until mixture is stiff and shiny.
- Carefully fold egg whites into lemon and cream mixture until completely incorporated.
- Spoon into prepared soufflé dish. Swirl top using back of spoon or spatula. Carefully cover top with foil. Freeze until firm (about 6 hours). Remove cover and garnish with mint leaves (when available). Remove from freezer 1 hour before serving.

Resolutions

Calypso
De La Cuisine
Bella Italia
Orient Express
Dessert Party
500 Calories (Plus or Minus) Dinner

Chapter Four A: Resolutions

Calypso
De La Cuisine
Bella Italia
Orient Express
Dessert Party
500 Calories (Plus or Minus) Dinner

Resolutions

It never fails that we resolve with the coming of the new year to take that most wanted trip sometime during the next twelve months. Unfortunately, with today's high costs, especially surrounding the luxury of travel, this desire usually remains unresolved.

Someone once said that it is not the travel which broadens one—it's all that foreign food! So true. But if you can't travel to that special far-away country this year, why not bring part of its beauty home to you and to your friends? Plan a zesty Italian dinner with at least five courses, and make the pasta yourself. Or, invite in your very close friends for the most intimate of French cuisine. A group effort in the kitchen can be fun while you sip your Saki and create an exciting Oriental dinner.

We have several foreign menus in this section which are easily prepared with everyday available foods. Choose one and set out on your trip, and make sure that you complement your dinner with the appropriate accents. Refer to magazines and travel brochures for extra details; your local travel agent may give you posters showing scenes of your dream country. With a little time and creativity, you can easily put together all the elements which set the mood for a delightful evening. Outside it may be snowing and blowing, as only it can around Georgian Bay, but inside you can create whatever dream world you wish.

To some people in the Georgian Bay region, the first few months of the new year can be rather cold and gray, and downright depressing. Often it feels like winter will never end. However, we found a way to combat those winter 'blahs': we put together some of our favourite recipes and held a Dessert Party for 50 of our female friends. It provided a delightful interlude to those dreary months and gave us the opportunity to visit together while enjoying a special selection of sweet treats. If you choose to have a dessert party, try to put all the desserts out on display for your guests to see, and don't worry about not having enough to go around: your friends will only want a small sample of each because of the richness of these desserts.

Nevertheless, enjoying exotic foreign foods and sweet desserts can eventually catch up with you. Many of us must once again make that age-old resolution to lose weight. But, dieting doesn't mean you have to withdraw from the world; your friends are probably feeling the same way after the Christmas and New Year's festivities. So, do yourself a favour; plan interesting diet meals and invite your fellow dieters over for a delicious low-cal dinner. (Try the one in this chapter.) Get lots of exercise, the kind that keeps your thoughts and hands away from the refrigerator. Plan to ski, go for brisk walks, or even schedule a round of exercises at home (in lieu of cocktails) before dinner.

May we suggest that you make at least one resolution: try the recipes in our Resolutions chapter, for they are sure to please any palate.

Special Party Punch, page 97. Katies Grand Torte, page 101. Orange Butter Cookies, page 99.

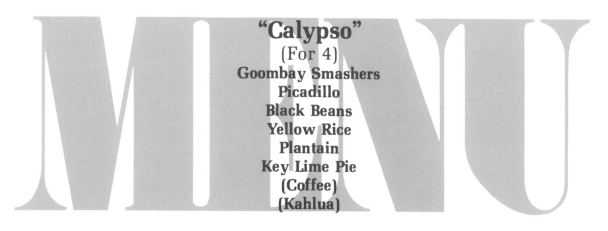

"Calypso"
(For 4)
Goombay Smashers
Picadillo
Black Beans
Yellow Rice
Plantain
Key Lime Pie
(Coffee)
(Kahlua)

Goombay Smashers
(Serves 1)

1¼ oz. rum   ¼ cup lemon juice
3 oz. pineapple juice   ¾ oz. coconut rum

- Combine ingredients and pour over crushed ice.

Picadillo
(Serves 4)

2 onions, chopped
1 green pepper, chopped   ¼ cup green stuffed olives
1 clove garlic, crushed   ½ cup raisins
1 tbsp. oil   2 tbsp. capers
1 14oz. can tomatoes   1 tbsp. vinegar
1 lb. ground beef   salt and pepper to taste

- Sauté onions, pepper and garlic in oil until tender.
- Stir in tomatoes and meat.
- Add olives, raisins, capers, vinegar, salt and pepper. Cook slowly until meat is tender, approximately 1 hour.

Preparation Note: Just as good reheated the next day.

Black Beans
(Serves 4)

1 lb. (2⅓ cups) black beans   2 cloves garlic
4 tbsp. olive oil   salt and pepper
2 onions, chopped   1 bay leaf
1 green pepper, chopped   3 tbsp. vinegar

- Rinse beans and cover with water. Soak overnight.
- In morning, simmer beans in same water until tender.
- In oil, fry onions, pepper and garlic until tender.
- Add to beans along with salt, pepper, bay leaf and vinegar. Cook slowly, stirring frequently to prevent sticking.
- Mash beans occasionally to thicken.

Preparation Note: Just as good when reheated.

Yellow Rice
(Serves 4)

2 cups water
1 cup rice
1 tsp. saffron

3 slices cooked ham
3 strips diced pimiento

- Bring water to a boil.
- Add rice and saffron. Follow cooking directions on rice package.
- Dice ham and fry until crisp.
- Add ham and garnish with diced pimiento.

Preparation Note: Saffron is expensive and hard to find. We often substitute with tumeric.

Plantain
(Serves 4)

2 plantain   2 tbsp. oil

- Peel plantain and slice diagonally, about 1″ thick.
- Place in oil and brown.
- Turn, mash down, and brown.

Preparation Note: If plantain is unavailable, slightly under-ripe bananas can be used.

Key Lime Pie
(Serves 6, Oven 325°)

4 eggs, separated
1 14oz. can sweetened condensed milk

⅓ cup lime juice
9″ baked pie shell (see Basics, page 212)

- Beat the egg yolks with one of the egg whites until thick.
- Add condensed milk and beat.
- Add lime juice and beat until thick.
- Beat remaining egg whites until dry and fold into mixture.
- Pour into a baked pie shell and cook about 15 minutes until set.

MENU

"De La Cuisine"
(For 4)
Soupe à L'Oignon
Poulet avec Raisins Blancs
Asperges de Citron
Carottes au Sirop
Baguettes
Crème Caramel

Soupe à L'Oignon
(Serves 4)

3 large cooking onions, coarsely chopped
¼ cup oil
½ tsp. thyme
1 bay leaf

1 cup dry red wine
3 cups beef consommé (See Basics, page 207)
4 slices dry French bread
¼ lb. grated Swiss cheese

- Sauté onion in oil until transparent.
- Add thyme and bay leaf; stir in wine. Allow to boil for a few minutes. Add consommé and cook uncovered for 20 minutes.
- Pour soup into 4 large ovenproof soup bowls. Top each with a slice of French bread. Sprinkle with cheese. Broil quickly until bubbling and golden. Serve at once.

Poulet avec Raisins Blancs
(Serves 4, Oven 350°)

¼ lb. uncooked ham, diced
¼ cup water
4 chicken breasts
1 tsp. salt
¼ tsp. pepper
1 tbsp. oil
3 tbsp. butter

1 lb. potatoes, peeled and sliced thickly
2 tbsp. flour
2 cups cream (half and half)
1 cup white table wine
¼ lb. fresh mushrooms, sliced
1 cup seedless grapes

- Simmer ham in water for 15 minutes. Drain.
- Season chicken with salt and pepper. In a skillet brown in oil and 1 tbsp. of the butter. Remove to a casserole.
- Brown potatoes in fat remaining in skillet and add to casserole.
- In a saucepan melt remaining butter. Blend in flour and cook 1 minute. Add cream and wine and stir until smooth and thick.
- Add ham and mushrooms to casserole and season to taste.
- Pour cream-wine sauce over mixture in casserole and bake for 30 minutes.
- Add grapes and bake 10 minutes more.

Asperges de Citron
(Serves 4)

1 lb. fresh asparagus, cooked   1 tbsp. lemon juice
2 tbsp. melted butter

- Arrange hot cooked asparagus in heated serving dish.
- Combine melted butter and lemon juice, pour over asparagus. Serve hot.

Carottes au Sirop
(Serves 4)

12 medium carrots, cut in olive shapes   black pepper
1½ cups chicken stock (see Basics,   1 tbsp. dill weed
   page 207)   1 tbsp. fresh parsley, finely chopped
4 tbsp. butter
2 tbsp. brown sugar
½ tsp. salt

- Combine carrots, stock, butter, brown sugar, salt and touch of pepper in an 8 to 10" skillet. Bring to boil over moderate heat.
- Reduce to a low heat. Cover pan and simmer for 25 minutes, shaking pan frequently to coat the carrots with the sauce. Carrots should be tender but not soft, and the sauce a brown syrup. (If the sauce is not thick enough remove the carrots and continue cooking liquid over medium heat.)
- To serve, stir carrots in syrup to cover. Transfer carrots to a heated serving dish and sprinkle with dill and parsley.

Baguettes
(Yields 3 loaves, Oven 400°)

1 heaping tbsp. butter   ⅔ cup lukewarm water
1 heaping tbsp. salt   approximately 6-6½ cups unbleached hard
1 heaping tbsp. sugar   wheat flour
2 cups boiling water   yellow corn meal
1 tbsp. dry yeast

- In a very large bowl combine butter, salt, sugar and 2 cups boiling water. Stir to dissolve; set aside to cool.
- Sprinkle yeast over ⅔ cup lukewarm water; set aside for 10 minutes.
- When butter mixture is lukewarm and yeast is foamy, combine.
- Add flour a little at a time. When 4 cups have been added and dough is beginning to get quite thick, beat vigorously for 10 minutes with a wooden spoon.
- Continue to add flour until dough is too stiff to mix with a spoon.
- Turn out onto a large floured board and knead, adding more flour as necessary until satiny smooth and very elastic.

con't next page

con't

- Form into a ball and place in a buttered bowl. Turn dough over so that the entire surface is buttered. Cover with Saran wrap or a tea towel. Place in a warm spot to rise for 1½ hours; the dough should be double in size.
- Punch down and let rise again until doubled; this time it should only take one hour.
- Grease baking dish with shortening and sprinkle lightly with corn meal.
- Divide dough into 3 equal portions and shape each into a long slender loaf. Do this by rolling out each portion into a rectangle about 14"-15" long and 10" wide. Roll up long side of rectangle tightly until it is a narrow even loaf 1½" wide. Seal the seam and ends by pinching. Place the 3 loaves on the prepared baking sheet. Cover with a dry tea towel and let rise until nearly double in size—approximately 45 minutes.
- Brush tops of loaves with cold water. With a very sharp knife, make 3 or 4 diagonal slashes across top of each loaf.
- Place a shallow pan of hot water in lower part of oven. Bake loaves 45 to 60 minutes. Brush tops and sides of loaves with cold water every 15 to 20 minutes. This makes the crisp and hard crust for which French bread is so famous.

Crème Caramel
(Serves 4-6, Oven 325°)

Caramel
1 cup sugar
¼ cup water
pinch of cream of tartar

- Caramelize sugar by placing it in a heavy saucepan with the water. Bring to a boil over high heat, stirring until sugar has dissolved. Add cream of tartar. Reduce heat to medium and continue to boil, constantly tipping the pot back and forth until the syrup turns golden brown.
- Immediately place the caramel into ring mold or individual custard cups; tilt so the syrup evenly coats sides and bottom of mold. Work quickly.

Custard
5 eggs   1 tsp. vanilla
½ cup sugar   3½ cups of milk
¼ tsp. salt

- In large bowl with wire whisk beat eggs with sugar, salt and vanilla to mix well.
- Gradually add milk beating until smooth, not frothy.
- Place prepared mold or cups in shallow pan. Pour egg mixture into mold or cups.
- Place baking pan on middle rack in oven. Pour hot water into pan about 1" deep. Bake 55 to 60 minutes or until inserted knife comes out clean. (Do not overbake as custard continues to bake after removal from pan). Remove mold from hot water to cool completely. Chill in refrigerator for 2 to 3 hours. (Can be made a day ahead).
- To serve, loosen edge with spatula. Place serving plate upside down on mold and invert. Shake gently to release. Serve chilled.

MENU

"Bella Italia"
(For 4)
Prosciutto con Mellone
Stracciatella
Fettuccine al Burro
Scaloppine al Limone
Pomodori Ripieni
Insalata di Funghi Crudi
Zabaione
(Formaggio e Frutta)
(Cheese and Fruit)
(Espresso)

Prosciutto con Mellone
(Prosciutto with melon)

(Serves 4)

2 small honeydew melons
8 oz. prosciutto or parma ham, sliced extremely thin

- Chill melons.
- Cut each melon into 8 wedges and remove seeds. Slice away skin from each wedge.
- Place 2 pieces of melon on each plate and drape slices of prosciutto over melon.

Stracciatella
(Chicken soup with flakes of egg and cheese)

(Serves 4)

2 eggs, slightly beaten
2 tbsp. grated Parmesan cheese
2 tsp. finely chopped fresh parsley

pinch of nutmeg
pinch of salt
1 quart Chicken Stock (see Basics, page 207)

- Mix together eggs, cheese, parsley, nutmeg and salt.
- In a large heavy saucepan, bring chicken stock to a rapid boil.
- Pour in egg mixture, stirring gently and constantly with a whisk. The egg and cheese mixture should form tiny flakes.
- Simmer 2 to 3 minutes, stirring frequently.
- Season to taste. Serve immediately.

Homemade Fettuccine
(Serves 4)

1½ cups flour, unsifted

1 egg

1 egg white

1 tbsp. olive oil

1 tsp. salt

few drops of water

- Place flour in a mound on a pastry board and make a well in the centre.
- Break eggs into well; add oil, salt and fill in well with flour from the sides of the mound.
- Work the mixture with your hands until it forms a ball. If the mixture is too dry (it should be crumbly to begin with) add a few drops of water. Knead for 10 minutes. It should be smooth, elastic and shiny. Divide into 2 parts.
- Dust each part and roll each into a paper thin sheet.
- Roll each thin sheet into a long jelly roll shape.
- Cut each roll into ¼" strips and quickly unroll to avoid sticking together.
- Cook at once, or wrap tightly in Saran and refrigerate for no longer than 24 hours.

Fettuccine al Burro
(Egg noodles with butter and cheese)
(Serves 4)

8 tbsp. butter

¼ cup whipping cream

½ cup grated Parmesan cheese

7 quarts water

1 tbsp. salt

1 lb. fettuccine, homemade or packaged

1 can white truffles, finely chopped
(optional)

- Cream butter in a heavy bowl until fluffy.
- Beat in cream a few tablespoons at a time.
- Add grated cheese. Beat 30 seconds. Cover bowl and set aside over hot water to keep warm.
- Bring water and salt to a boil in a very large pot.
- Drop in fettuccine and stir for a moment to prevent the strands from sticking.
- Boil, stirring occasionally 5 to 7 minutes. (It should be "al dente"—tender yet resistant to the bite, but not too soft.)
- Thoroughly drain fettuccine. Transfer at once to a warm serving bowl.
- Add butter and cheese mixture and toss to coat each strand.
- Season to taste, stir in truffles.
- Serve at once and offer grated Parmesan to sprinkle on top.

Scaloppine al Limone
(Sautéed veal scallops with lemon)
(Serves 4)

1½ lbs. veal scallops (have the butcher cut them and pound them to ¼ inch thick)
salt and pepper
¼ cup flour
2 tbsp. butter

3 tbsp. olive oil
¾ cup Beef Stock (see Basics, page 207)
lemon slices, cut paper thin
1 tbsp. lemon juice
2 tbsp. soft butter

- Dust veal scallops with salt, pepper and flour.
- In a large skillet, melt butter and oil over medium heat.
- Add a few veal scallops at a time and sauté 2 minutes on each side, or until golden brown. Remove slices to a plate and keep warm.
- Pour off most of the fat from pan, leaving only a thin film on the bottom and add ½ cup of Beef Stock. Boil 1 to 2 minutes and scrape in browned bits from bottom and sides.
- Return veal to pan and arrange lemon slices on top. Cover and simmer over low heat for 10 minutes.
- Transfer veal to serving platter and surround with lemon slices. Add remaining Beef Stock to juices in pan and boil until stock becomes a thick syrup. Add lemon juice; cook and stir 1 minute.
- Remove pan from heat, swirl in the soft butter. Drip sauce over scallops. Serve immediately.

Pomodori Ripieni
(Stuffed Tomatoes)
(Serves 4, Oven 375°)

4 medium tomatoes
6½ oz. can tuna fish
3 slices bread, coarsely crumbled, (crusts removed)
8 anchovy fillets, chopped

1 clove garlic, crushed
½ tsp. dried basil
2 tbsp. fine dry breadcrumbs
1½ tbsp. grated Parmesan cheese
3 tbsp. melted butter

- Cut tops off tomatoes and discard. Scoop out pulp and push through a sieve into a medium bowl.
- Add tuna, crumbled bread, anchovy fillets, garlic and basil and mix well.
- Stuff each hollowed tomato with mixture.
- Combine bread crumbs, cheese and melted butter and sprinkle over stuffed tomatoes.
- Arrange tomatoes in baking dish and bake 20 minutes or until golden brown and heated through.

Insalata di Funghi Crudi
(Raw mushroom salad)
(Serves 4)

½ lb. fresh mushrooms, sliced very thin   3 tbsp. olive oil
2 tsp. lemon juice   ½ tsp. salt
¼ cup scallion greens, sliced very thin

- Toss mushrooms with lemon juice until slices are lightly coated.
- Add scallion greens, oil and salt, and toss again.
- Chill well and serve.

Preparation Note: When scallion greens are unavailable, use greens of green onions.

Zabaione
(Custard with Marsala)
(Serves 4)

5 egg yolks   2 tbsp. sugar
1 egg   ½ cup Marsala

- Combine egg yolks, egg and sugar in the top of a double boiler above simmering water.
- Beat mixture with a whisk until fluffy and pale yellow in colour.
- Gradually add Marsala and continue beating, as long as 10 minutes, or until mixture becomes thick enough to hold its shape in a spoon.
- Divide mixture into individual dessert bowls or large stemmed glasses and serve while it is still hot.

MENU

Orient Express
(For 6)

Corn Soup
Egg Rolls
Sweet and Sour Pork
Chicken and Cashews
String Beans and Almonds
(White Rice)
Fruit in Melon

Please Note: If you prepare the whole menu it will serve 6. But, individually, some of these recipes will not serve 6.

Corn Soup
(Serves 6)

bones of 4 chicken breasts (from Chicken
  and Cashew recipe, page 95)
6 cups cold water
½ tsp. salt
2 medium onions, finely chopped
1 cup celery, finely diced

2 chicken bouillon cubes
salt and pepper to taste
dash of tabasco
1 10oz. can creamed corn

- In large soup kettle combine chicken bones, cold water and salt. Bring to a boil. Simmer ½ hour. Skim off any foam.
- Add onion and celery and simmer for 1 hour.
- Remove bones from kettle and remove any meat from the bones. Return meat to broth and add chicken bouillon cubes. Stir until dissolved. Add salt and pepper to taste. (If broth doesn't have enough flavour, add another cube).
- Add a dash of tabasco and creamed corn. Simmer over low heat until ready to serve.

Eggrolls

(Yields approximately 20 eggrolls)

½ small cabbage, finely shredded
½ lb. ground beef
2 small onions, finely diced
1 clove garlic, crushed
½ cup mushrooms, finely chopped

1 tbsp. soy sauce
tabasco to taste
salt and pepper to taste
eggroll wrappers
½ cup oil

Paste
1 tbsp. flour
few drops of water

- Steam shredded cabbage for 5 minutes. If you don't have a steamer, boil in water about 5 mins. but drain very well. Set aside.
- Stir-fry beef in a bit of oil until browned. Add onions, crushed garlic and chopped mushrooms. Fry a few minutes longer.
- Add drained cabbage to meat mixture and mix well.
- Add soy sauce and a few drops of tabasco. Season with salt and pepper. Let cool.
- When mixture has cooled, wrap in eggroll wrappers. Seal wrappers with a bit of the flour and water paste. Set aside on a plate until you are ready to fry.
- Cover bottom of frying pan with oil, and fry eggrolls until they are golden on each side. Drain on paper towel and keep warm in oven until ready to serve.

Serving Suggestion: Place small dishes of plum sauce, hot mustard or cocktail sauce on the table for the eggroll dip.

Sweet and Sour Pork

(Serves 4 individually, 6 in dinner)

1 lb. lean pork
1 recipe Marinade (next page)
½ cup cornstarch
½ cup oil
1 medium onion, sliced

2 celery sticks, sliced
1 recipe Sweet and Sour Sauce (next page)
1 tomato cut in wedges
1 10oz. can pineapple chunks

- Cut pork into bite sized pieces.
- Combine Marinade ingredients (below) and marinate pork for ½ hour.
- Pour cornstarch into a shallow pan and coat each piece of pork.
- Heat ¼ cup oil in wok or frying pan and stir-fry pork, a few pieces at a time. Remove pieces as they brown after 2 to 3 minutes and set aside. Once all pieces are browned, drain oil from pan. Heat remaining ¼ cup fresh oil in wok; fry pork once again until crispy. Remove pork and keep warm in oven. Drain oil from wok leaving about 1 table-spoon.
- Stir-fry onions and celery for 2 to 3 minutes.
- Combine ingredients for Sweet and Sour Sauce (below). Add sauce to celery and onions in wok. Stir until thickened.
- Add pork to wok mixture and heat well.
- Decorate mixture with tomato wedges and pineapple chunks. Serve immediately.

Serving Suggestion: Serve with rice cooked according to package directions.

Marinade:

½ tsp. salt
½ tsp. soy sauce
1 tbsp. cornstarch

1 tbsp. water
1 egg
⅛ tsp. ginger

Sweet and Sour Sauce:

½ cup water
¼ cup vinegar
1 tbsp. soy sauce

¼ cup ketchup
2 tsp. cornstarch
2½ tbsp. brown sugar

Chicken and Cashews

(Serves 4 individually, 6 in dinner)

4 chicken breasts
⅛ tsp. ginger
1 chicken bouillon cube
1 cup hot water
2 tbsp. oil
1 cup celery, diagonally sliced

1 large onion, sliced
4 oz. cashew nuts
1 tsp. soy sauce
dash tabasco
1 tbsp. cornstarch to thicken

- Bone chicken. Set bones aside for the Corn Soup (see page 93).
- Cut chicken into bite-sized pieces. Set aside in a bowl and sprinkle with ginger.
- Dissolve bouillon cube in 1 cup of hot water.
- Heat oil in wok or frying pan and stir-fry chicken for 3 to 4 minutes.
- Add celery and onion, stirring constantly for another 3 to 4 minutes.
- Stir in cashew nuts.
- Add broth, soy sauce, tabasco and bring to a boil.
- Dissolve cornstarch in a bit of water and add cornstarch mixture to the chicken to thicken. Boil, stirring constantly 2 to 3 minutes.
- Serve immediately.

String Beans and Almonds

(Serves 4 individually, 6 in dinner — Oven 350°)

¼ cup slivered almonds
1 10oz. pkg. cooked frozen string beans

1 tbsp. butter
salt and pepper

- Toast slivered almonds in the oven on a cookie sheet for 1 to 2 minutes.
- Place beans in a serving dish and toss with butter, salt and pepper.
- Top with toasted almonds and serve immediately.

Fruit in Melon
(Serves 6)

A watermelon is best for this recipe, but if they are not in season you can use both halves of any melon in season or cut a pineapple in half.

1 melon or pineapple	kumquats
Mandarin oranges	melon balls
bananas	peaches
pineapple chunks	cherries
grapes	pears
lychees	

- Using a large knife, cut off the top of the melon lengthwise. Scallop top of melon. If you use a honeydew melon, cut in half, if you use a pineapple cut in ½ lengthwise and use both halves to serve fruit in. Remove pulp.
- Cut melon fruit or pineapple into squares or balls.
- In a large bowl combine your favourite fruits to equal approximately 6 cups of fruit.
- Place fruit in melon or pineapple half and chill well before serving.

Dessert Party
Special Party Punch
Chilly Chocolate Squares
Crème de Menthe Torte
Orange Butter Cookies
Zuppa Inglese
Chocolate Cheese Cake
Old Fashioned Apple Pie
Chocolate Mousse
Katie's Grand Torte
Sunshine Cake
Amaretto Roll
$300 Carrot Cake
(Coffee and Tea)
(Mints)

Special Party Punch
(Yields 36 cups)

6 tbsp. sugar
24 whole allspice
6-8 short cinnamon sticks
16 cups cranberry juice cocktail

6 26oz. bottles white sparkling wine
½ cup Amaretto liqueur
1 recipe Frosted Grapes for garnish (below)

Morning Before:
- Combine sugar, allspice, cinnamon and 4 cups cranberry juice in a large pot. Bring to a boil.
- Reduce heat, cover and simmer for 10 minutes.
- Cover and refrigerate.
- Prepare Frosted Grapes.

Frosted Grapes:
2 lbs. seedless grapes
4 egg whites

½ cup sugar

- Break grapes into small clusters.
- Beat egg whites until frothy.
- Dip each cluster in egg white, then into sugar. Allow to dry on a wire rack.

To Serve:
- Strain cranberry juice mixture into a large punch bowl (discard spices).
- Add remaining cranberry juice, champagne and Amaretto liqueur.
- Garnish with Frosted Grapes.

Chilly Chocolate Squares
(Yields 1½ dozen squares)

½ cup light cream
2 6oz. pkgs. semi-sweet chocolate chips
½ tsp. vanilla
2 cups graham cracker crumbs
½ cup icing sugar
½ cup chopped nuts

¼ cup butter
2 cups icing sugar
2 tbsp. milk
1½ tsp. peppermint flavouring
2 tbsp. water

- In a saucepan combine cream and 1 pkg. of chips and place over low heat until chips have melted.
- Remove from heat and add vanilla.
- In another bowl, combine graham cracker crumbs, ½ cup icing sugar and nuts.
- Add chocolate mixture to crumb mixture and mix together.
- Press this mixture evenly into a 9"x9" pan and chill.
- Beat together the butter, 2 cups icing sugar, milk and peppermint flavouring. Spread this like an icing on chilled crumb mixture in pan. Chill again.
- Melt remaining package of chocolate chips mixed with water and stir until smooth.
- Drizzle chocolate glaze in a criss-cross pattern over squares.
- Chill several hours.

Crème de Menthe Torte

This torte must be prepared in advance.

90-95 large marshmallows (1 lb. 2 oz.)
¾ cup green crème de menthe
Garnish—Chocolate Scrolls (below)

2 cups whipping cream
22 lady fingers approx. 3" in size

- Melt marshmallows with crème de menthe in a large saucepan over very low heat. Stir occasionally. Do not allow it to boil. When melted, remove from heat and cool.
- Whip cream until it mounds lightly (not stiff). Remove 1 cup and reserve for topping. Pour cooled marshmallow mixture over the remainder and fold in until completely blended.
- Arrange ladyfingers vertically around the sides of a 9" spring form pan, sugar side next to metal. (They stand better if not separated.)
- Pour filling into lined pan.
- Spread reserved whipped cream over top and garnish with Chocolate Scrolls (below). Seal with plastic wrap and refrigerate at least 6 hours (overnight is best).
- Remove rim from pan, place torte on serving tray and present to guests before cutting. (It cuts easily and holds shape well.)

Chocolate Scrolls:
1 oz. semi-sweet chocolate (1 square)

Let chocolate square stand in warm place until softened. Draw a vegetable peeler carefully across flat side. Chocolate will come off in curls. If this doesn't happen, the chocolate is not soft enough. Do this over a dinner plate and chill a few minutes until hardened enough for handling. Lift with spatula and scatter over torte.

Orange Butter Cookies
(Yields 3 dozen, Oven 375°)

½ cup butter

1 cup sugar

2 egg yolks

1 tbsp. orange juice

grated rind of half an orange

1½ cups flour

¼ tsp. salt

1 tsp. baking powder

- Cream butter. Beat in sugar, egg yolks, orange juice and rind.
- Sift together flour, salt and baking powder and mix into butter mixture.
- Chill in refrigerator 3 to 4 hours.
- With a teaspoon, roll dough into small balls. Place on greased cookie sheet; flatten slightly with a knife and bake 8 to 10 minutes.
- Optional: Brush cookies with melted butter while still warm.

Zuppa Inglese
(Serves 10-12)

This is an Italian wine cake covered with custard like an English Trifle. It should be made a day in advance and kept in freezer.

1 recipe Custard Filling (below)

1 Butter Sponge Cake (see Basics, page 208), prepared in bundt pan, tube mold or spring form with tube centre

1 cup sherry

⅔ cup currant jelly

1 recipe Topping (below)

- Prepare Custard Filling (below).
- Cut cake horizontally into 3 layers. Place bottom layer on a serving plate, sprinkle it with ⅓ cup sherry and spread it with ⅓ cup currant jelly and a layer of the cooled custard. Repeat with second layer, then top with third layer. Sprinkle top layer with remaining ⅓ cup of sherry.
- Prepare Topping (below).
- Place cake in freezer. Remove 1 hour before serving.

Custard Filling:

2 cups milk

4 egg yolks

7 tbsp. flour

grated rind of 1 lemon

¾ cup sugar

1 tbsp. cornstarch

- In a saucepan, scald milk.
- Mix egg yolks, flour, lemon rind, sugar and cornstarch. Beat well.
- Add a little of the hot milk to the egg mixture; beat. Gradually add all mixture to the egg mixture.
- Place mixture in a double boiler and cook over hot water until thickened. Stir constantly. Do not allow to boil. Cool.

Topping:

1½ cups whipping cream

2 tbsp. rum

3 tbsp. ground pistachio nuts

- Whip cream until stiff. Stir in rum.
- Spread cream over top and sides of cake. Sprinkle cake with ground pistachio nuts.

Chocolate Cheese Cake
(Oven 350°)

18 chocolate wafers
¼ cup butter, melted
¼ tsp. cinnamon
1½ lbs. cream cheese, softened
1 cup sugar

3 eggs
8 oz. semi-sweet chocolate, melted
2 tsp. cocoa
1 tsp. vanilla
2 cups sour cream
whipped cream

- Crush wafers, mix with butter and cinnamon, press into the bottom of a 9″ spring form pan. Chill.
- In a large bowl beat cream cheese until light and fluffy.
- Beat in sugar and add eggs, one at a time, beating well after each addition.
- Beat in the melted chocolate, cocoa, and vanilla, blending thoroughly.
- Beat in sour cream and pour mixture over crumb base.
- Bake 1 hour and 10 minutes.
- The cake will be runny but will firm as it chills. Cool at room temperature and then chill in refrigerator for at least 6 hours or overnight.
- Garnish with whipped cream.

Preparation Note: Cake sometimes cracks on top.

Old Fashioned Apple Pie
(Serves 6-8, Oven 425°)

1 pie shell, 9″ or 10″ (see Basics, page 212)

½-1 cup sugar (depending on tartness
   of apples)
2 tbsp. flour
pinch of cinnamon *or* nutmeg

6-7 medium sized cooking apples
¼ cup cheddar cheese, grated
1 recipe Topping (below)

- Combine sugar, flour and cinnamon.
- Slice half of the peeled apples into pie shell and sprinkle half of the flour-sugar mixture over the apples.
- Slice remaining apples and sprinkle the rest of flour mixture over the top.
- Sprinkle grated cheese over the apples.

Topping
1¼ cup flour   ½ cup butter
⅓ cup brown sugar, packed

- Combine ingredients and mix with pastry blender until mixture resembles coarse crumbs.
- Pack firmly over the cheese on the pie.
- Bake at 425° for 10 minutes. Reduce heat to 350° and bake 40 minutes. Topping may brown very quickly in which case put some foil over the top of pie.

Chocolate Mousse

2 cups semi-sweet chocolate chips
  (12oz. package)
10 tbsp. boiling water
8 egg yolks

4 tbsp. rum or brandy
8 egg whites
Garnish—toasted almonds, pecans,
  coconut or whipping cream

- Put chips in blender or food processor and process at high speed for 6 seconds.
- Scrape down the sides and add boiling water and blend for another 10 seconds.
- Add egg yolks and liqueur and blend 3 seconds more until smooth.
- Beat egg whites until stiff but not dry and fold into chocolate mixture.
- Spoon into serving dishes, glasses or serving bowl. Chill at least one hour and garnish before serving.

Garnish with toasted almonds, pecans, coconut or whipped cream.

Katie's Grand Torte

(Serves 10, Oven 350°)

½ cup butter
1⅔ cup sugar
3 eggs
1 tsp. vanilla
1¾ cups flour
1 tsp. baking soda

1 tsp. baking powder
1 tsp. salt
½ cup cocoa
1⅓ cups water
¼ cup Grand Marnier
1 recipe Grand Marnier Filling (below)

- In a large bowl cream butter, gradually adding sugar, beating until light and fluffy.
- Beat in eggs one at a time; add vanilla and beat well.
- Sift together dry ingredients. Add ⅓ of the flour mixture to the cream mixture, add half the water, repeat ending with the remaining flour.
- Turn into two 8″ round well greased cake pans. Bake 25 to 30 minutes or until centre of cake springs back when lightly touched. Cool cakes thoroughly on racks.
- Two hours before assembling, cut each cake in half, place layers cut side up on waxed paper and sprinkle with Grand Marnier.

Grand Marnier Filling

4 oz. frozen orange juice concentrate,
  unsweetened
¾ cup sugar
1 tbsp. gelatin (1 envelope)
grated peel of 2 oranges

¼ cup Grand Marnier
3 cups whipping cream
¾ cup sifted icing sugar

- Cook orange juice, sugar and gelatin in saucepan over medium heat. Stir constantly until sugar and gelatin are dissolved (approximately 5 minutes).
- Remove from heat and stir in orange peel and Grand Marnier. Cover surface with waxed paper and refrigerate until it no longer feels warm to touch (20 minutes).
- Whip cream in a large bowl until it forms soft peaks. Gradually beat in icing sugar. Fold in Grand Marnier mixture.
- To assemble, place one layer of cake cut side up on serving plate. Spoon some of the filling onto the middle of layer and gently spread almost to the edge. Top with next layer and repeat until all layers are used.
- Refrigerate immediately, let set 4 hours for flavours to blend.

Preparation Note: Cake can be prepared the day before if stored in tight container.

Sunshine Cake
(Oven 275°-300°)

4 eggs separated
1 tsp. cold water
1½ cups sugar
⅔ cup boiling water
1½ cups all purpose flour

1 tsp. baking powder
½ tsp. salt
½ tsp. cream of tartar
1 tsp. vanilla
1 recipe Whipped Cream Chocolate Topping (below)

- Beat egg yolks with cold water until thick and frothy.
- Add sugar gradually. Add boiling water and beat.
- Sift all purpose flour with baking powder and add salt. Sift these dry ingredients 3 times again. Fold into egg mixture.
- Beat egg whites with cream of tartar until stiff. Fold into mixture. Add vanilla and blend gently.
- Bake in ungreased angel cake pan for 45 to 60 minutes or until cake is golden and springs back to the touch.
- Allow cake to cool in pan upside down, on a cooling rack. (If cake is prepared ahead of time, loosen edges of cooled cake with a knife. Refrigerate cake in pan until a few hours before serving. Slice cake in half horizontally to make two layers. Ice with Whipped Cream Chocolate Topping.)

Whipped Cream Chocolate Topping
3 tbsp. cocoa
1 cup icing sugar
2 cups whipping cream

- Sift cocoa and icing sugar together.
- Fold into unwhipped cream and refrigerate until ready to ice cake.
- Whip and spread mixture generously between layers and over top and sides of cake.

Preparation Note: This cake is best when prepared a day ahead and kept in the refrigerator until serving time. Ice just before serving.

Amaretto Roll
(Oven 375°)

Cake
4 egg yolks
¾ cup sugar
3 tbsp. Amaretto liqueur
¾ cup sifted flour

1 tsp. baking powder
½ tsp. salt
4 egg whites
1 recipe Filling (see next page)
icing sugar

- Butter a 12″ x 14″ jellyroll pan or cookie sheet with sides; line with waxed paper and butter again.
- In mixing bowl beat egg yolks until thick and lemon coloured (about 5 minutes).
- Add sugar and beat 2 minutes longer.
- Add Amaretto liqueur and beat.
- Sift flour before measuring, measure and resift with baking powder and salt.
- Gradually add flour to egg and sugar mixture; beat until smooth.

- In a separate bowl, beat egg whites until stiff but not too dry; fold egg whites lightly into batter.
- Pour mixture in jellyroll pan, spread evenly with a spatula and bake for 12 minutes.
- Loosen sides of cake and turn out onto towel sprinkled with sifted icing sugar. Trim off any hard edges.
- Roll quickly and wrap in towel; place on rack to cool.

(This much can be done a day ahead. Refrigerate.)

Filling

½ pint whipping cream
2 tbsp. Amaretto Liqueur

2 tbsp. sugar
1 cup crushed almonds

- Whip cream with Amaretto and sugar.
- Unroll cake and spread with cream.
- Sprinkle cream with crushed nuts.
- Reroll and chill until ready to serve. Slice.

Preparation Note: Completed roll can be made a few hours ahead and wrapped in plastic wrap and placed in fridge until needed.

$300 Carrot Cake

(Oven 300°)

1 cup sugar
1 cup oil
3 eggs
1½ cups flour
¾ tsp. salt
1⅓ tsp. baking powder

1 tsp. soda
1⅓ tsp. cinnamon
2 cups finely grated carrots
1 cup chopped Brazil nuts
1 tsp. grated Brazil nuts
1 recipe Icing (below)

- Beat together sugar and oil with mixer.
- Add eggs one at a time while continuing to beat.
- Sift flour, salt, baking powder, soda and cinnamon together and add to first mixture. Mix well.
- Fold in carrots and chopped Brazil nuts. Mix well.
- Pour into 2 round 8″ or 9″ greased cake pans and bake for 35 to 40 minutes.
- Cool for 5 minutes on rack and remove from pans to cool further.
- Ice cake and sprinkle with grated Brazil nuts.

Icing

8 oz. cream cheese, softened
⅛ lb. butter, softened

2 cups icing sugar
2 tsp. vanilla

- Cream cheese and butter well together.
- Add icing sugar and vanilla and blend well.

"500 Calories (Plus or Minus) Dinner"
(For 4)
Fruit Salad Platter
Diet Chilled Cucumber Soup
Beef Rollups
Celery Braised in Broth
Potato Pancakes
Peachy Strawberry Crêpes
(Tea with Lemon)

Fruit Salad Platter
(Serves 4, 50 Calories)

½ fresh pineapple, peeled and sliced
1 pint fresh strawberries (or frozen)
½ honeydew melon, made into balls
½ cantaloup, made into balls

1 peach, peeled and sliced (or canned)
1 apple, peeled and sliced
½ head of lettuce
1 recipe Yoghurt Dip (below)

• Prepare fruit. Arrange on a platter and place fresh fruit on lettuce.

Yoghurt Dips

1½ cups plain low fat yoghurt
½ mashed banana

1 tbsp. limeade concentrate
1 tbsp. orange juice concentrate

• Divide yoghurt into three ½ cup portions.
• Add mashed banana to ½ cup yoghurt.
• Add limeade concentrate to next ½ cup yoghurt.
• Add orange juice concentrate to remaining ½ cup yoghurt.

Serve dips with salad.

Diet Chilled Cucumber Soup
(Serves 4, 38 Calories)

2 cups chopped, seeded cucumber
1 tsp. salt
1 cup diet chicken broth
½ cup plain low fat yoghurt

1 tsp. lemon juice
¼ tsp. tabasco sauce
½ cup low fat cottage cheese

• Sprinkle the chopped cucumber with the salt and let stand for 15 minutes.
• Place all ingredients in a blender and blend until smooth.
• Chill.
• Serve in cold soup dishes with slivered cucumbers and fresh ground pepper for garnish.

Beef Rollups
(Serves 4, Oven 350°, 300 calories)

4 thin slices round steak
  (approximately ¾ lb.)
½ cup low fat cottage cheese
2 tbsp. grated Romano cheese
1 medium onion, minced
3 tbsp. chopped parsley
2 tsp. oregano

½ tsp. salt
½ clove garlic, minced
1 egg
1 cup tomato sauce
¼ cup dry red wine

- Trim fat off meat and flatten meat by rolling with a rolling pin or hammering with a meat mallet.
- Combine cheeses, onion, spices and egg in bowl.
- Spread the filling over the steak. Roll beef jellyroll fashion.
- Place rollups seam side down in a shallow baking dish just large enough to hold them.
- Combine tomato sauce and wine. Pour over beef rolls.
- Bake uncovered for 1 hour. Baste occasionally.

Celery Braised in Broth
(Serves 4, 20 calories)

1 onion sliced
1 carrot sliced

1 bunch celery, trimmed and sliced
2 cups diet chicken broth

- Place onion and carrots in skillet and arrange celery on top.
- Add broth to cover celery.
- Bring to a boil; lower heat and simmer about 45 minutes until tender.
- Drain and serve.

Potato Pancakes
(Serves 4, 200 calories)

1 cup shredded raw potatoes
1 egg beaten
salt

2 tbsp. grated onion
½ tbsp. flour
2 tbsp. diet margarine

- Combine all ingredients, except diet margarine, and stir to moisten.
- Cook in a non-stick skillet in diet margarine.
- Fry until crisp.

Peachy Strawberry Crêpes
(Serves 4, 100 calories)

1 recipe Crêpes (below)   1 recipe Filling (below)

Crêpes (Yields 6 large crêpes)
3 eggs   ½ cup skim milk
6 tbsp. flour   2 tbsp. diet margarine, melted

- Combine all ingredients, blending until smooth. Let rest for at least 20 minutes.
- If using a crêpe pan, grease with diet margarine. Rotate quickly in batter to coat pan. Cook about 40 seconds until surface of crêpe is dry. (A small non-stick fry pan may be used also.)
- Flip crêpe out of pan onto paper towelling.

Filling
1 cup fresh or frozen strawberries   ¼ cup orange juice
  without sugar   ½ cup low fat yoghurt
1 peach, peeled and sliced (or canned)   ½ cup low fat cottage cheese

- Combine strawberries and peach with orange juice. Chill several hours.
- Place yoghurt and cottage cheese in blender with liquid from peach mixture. Blend until smooth.
- On a serving dish, place 1 crêpe. Spread the fruit mixture and the yoghurt mixture on crêpe. Place a second crêpe on top and repeat procedure ending up with yoghurt and fruit on top.
- Cut in four to serve.

Preparation Note: Crêpes can also be rolled with fruit and yoghurt in each. Reserve some fruit and yoghurt mixture to top crêpes.

Skiing

Skiers' Reward
Après Ski Party
Beans 'N' Ribs
Mid-Day Energizers
Meal-In-One Soups
Heart Warmers
"It's Still Snowing . . . Why Don't You Stay For Dinner?"
(3 Menus)

Chapter Five: Skiing

Skiers' Reward
Après Ski Party
Beans 'N' Ribs
Mid-Day Energizers
Meal-In-One Soups
Heart Warmers
"It's Still Snowing . . . Why Don't You Stay For Dinner?"
(3 Menus)

Skiing

"There's no people like snow people . . ."

The Georgian Bay region is transformed into the winter wonderland of Ontario during the crisp winter months which make up the ski season. Thousands of ski enthusiasts flock to the many downhill and cross-country ski facilities in this area which are noted for their well groomed trails and excellent accommodations.

Consider the scene: clean, crisp air tugging at your lungs as you lean into the icy wind, propelling yourself downward, and plunging through the powdery snow . . . or . . . backpacking cross-country through a white fairyland forest with the rich smell of a log fire drifting through the pines. The scene is completed in a warm and cozy cabin nestled in the winterland of Georgian Bay and the finishing touches are revealed in this chapter. Here we present our favourite menus and recipes relating to fun-filled days of skiing adventures.

Skiers' Reward
(For 4)

Stuffed Cherry Tomatoes
Rib Ticklers
White Rice or Baked Potatoes
Orange and Cucumber Salad
Fruit Fondue
(Tea and Coffee)

Stuffed Cherry Tomatoes
(Serves 4)

1 pint cherry tomatoes
¼ cup low fat cottage cheese
1 tsp. chopped chives

salt and pepper to taste
3½ oz. tin smoked oysters
parsley sprigs for garnish

- Hollow tomatoes and turn upside down on paper towelling to drain.
- Mix cottage cheese, chives, salt and pepper to taste.
- Stuff half of the tomatoes with smoked oysters and the other half with the cottage cheese mixture.
- Decorate each tomato with a sprig of parsley and serve cold.

Rib Ticklers
(Serves 4, Oven 350°)

4 lbs. pork spareribs
½ cup honey
¼ cup soy sauce

1 cup ketchup
2 cloves of garlic, crushed

- Place ribs in a casserole. Cover and bake for 1¼ hours.
- Combine honey, soy sauce, ketchup and garlic.
- Pour sauce over ribs. Continue cooking half an hour or until tender. Turn ribs occasionally to coat with sauce.

Serving Suggestion: Nice served with rice or a baked potato topped with sour cream.

Orange and Cucumber Salad
(Serves 4)

1 seedless cucumber
1 can Mandarin orange segments
½ dozen radishes
1 tbsp. lemon juice

¼ tsp. salt
2 tbsp. olive oil
fresh parsley to garnish

- Slice cucumber thinly and place in bowl.
- Add drained Mandarin oranges and sliced radishes.
- Sprinkle with lemon juice, salt and olive oil. Toss thoroughly and serve at once.
- Garnish with fresh parsley.

Fruit Fondue
(Serves 4)

6 cups fresh fruit — apples, oranges,
   cherries, melon, bananas

1 recipe Cream Cheese Dip

Cream Cheese Dip

4 oz. cream cheese, softened
¼ cup sugar

1 tsp. vanilla
1 cup whipping cream

- Cream cheese with sugar and vanilla until light.
- Whip cream and fold in to cheese mixture. Refrigerate until ready to use.
- Arrange sections of fruit on a large platter and place dip in center.

Serving Suggestion: Give everyone a fondue fork. Dip fruit into the Cream Cheese Dip.

Après Ski Party
(For 4)
Swiss Fondue with French Bread
Roman Salad
Rich Pecan Pie
Café Claude

Swiss Fondue
(Serves 4)

½ lb. Gruyère or Emmenthaler cheese,
   grated
1½ tbsp. flour
1 cup dry white wine
1 clove garlic
¼-½ tsp. salt

⅛ tsp. pepper
dash of nutmeg (optional)
2 tbsp. Kirsch (optional)
French bread, broken into chunks

- Dredge the cheese with the flour.
- Pour wine into pan and set over low heat. Add clove of garlic to the wine.
- When wine is near boiling point, add cheese. Stir until cheese is completely melted and the mixture starts bubbling lightly.
- Add salt, pepper and nutmeg.
- Stir in Kirsch and mix thoroughly. Remove garlic.
- Set pan over a warmer to serve. Dunk bread into the cheese mixture.

Roman Salad
(Serves 4-6)

half of a large head of Iceberg lettuce
2 hard cooked eggs, sliced
½ cup chopped dill pickles
2 medium tomatoes, sliced and quartered
1 small onion, sliced in rings

⅓ cup vegetable oil
⅛ cup vinegar
1 tbsp. lemon juice
1 clove garlic, crushed
1 tsp. seasoned salt

- Combine lettuce, eggs, pickles, tomatoes and onion rings in a bowl.
- Combine oil, vinegar, lemon juice, garlic, seasoned salt and mix well.
- Pour oil mixture over lettuce and toss thoroughly. Serve at once.

Rich Pecan Pie
(Serves 6, Oven 425°)

¼ cup butter
1 cup brown sugar
¼ tsp. salt
1 cup corn syrup

3 eggs, beaten
1 tsp. vanilla
1½ cups pecan halves
1 9″ unbaked pie shell (see Basics, page 212)

- Cream butter and sugar.
- Add salt, corn syrup, eggs and vanilla; beat.
- Sprinkle pecans on bottom of pie shell.
- Pour filling over pecans.
- Bake at 425° for 10 minutes, reduce heat to 350° and bake approximately 35 minutes. Garnish with whipped cream.

Café Claude
(Serves 1)

1 tsp. sugar
1½ oz. whisky
5 oz. strong, hot coffee

1 tbsp. whipped heavy cream

- Warm an 8 oz. goblet or mug by rinsing in very hot water and shake to dry.
- Place sugar and whisky in glass; add the coffee and stir to dissolve sugar.
- Top with whipped cream.

Beans 'N' Ribs
(For 6)
Sweet and Sour Beans and Ribs
Turnip and Date Salad
Crescent Rolls
Apple Crisp

Sweet and Sour Beans and Ribs
(Serves 6, Oven 250°)

2 cups white beans
6 cups cold water
2 lb. midget spareribs (or back ribs
  cut up)
garlic powder and pepper to taste
2 onions, chopped
¼ cup cider vinegar

1 tbsp. dry mustard
¼ tsp. pepper
1 tbsp. salt
¼ cup brown sugar
¼ cup molasses
½ tsp. ground ginger

- Soak beans in water overnight. Next day, simmer until tender, about 1½ hours.
- Drain, reserving 2 cups of the liquid.
- Sprinkle spareribs with garlic powder and pepper and broil for 5 to 10 minutes, or, brown in a frying pan.
- Place meat, beans and onions in a bean pot.
- Combine remaining ingredients and pour over beans and ribs. Add the 2 cups of cooking liquid.
- Cover and bake for 4 hours. Remove cover for final 30 minutes of cooking time and increase heat to 350°, to form a crust.

Turnip and Date Salad
(Serves 6)

2 tart eating apples, peeled, cored and
  diced
2 tsp. lemon juice
1 medium sized turnip, peeled and
  finely grated
14 pitted dates, coarsely chopped

2 tsp. sugar
¼ cup light cream
1 small carrot, finely grated

- Place apples in medium-sized bowl and sprinkle with lemon juice.
- Add grated turnip and chopped dates and sprinkle with 1½ tsp. sugar. Combine thoroughly and gently.
- Pour in cream and toss the salad until the ingredients are thoroughly coated.
- Garnish the salad with grated carrot and sprinkle with remaining sugar. Serve at once.

Crescent Rolls
(Yields 2 doz., Oven 425°)

1 cup lukewarm milk
1 pkg. of yeast
2 tbsp. soft butter

1 tbsp. sugar
1 tsp. salt
2½ cups all purpose flour

- Place milk and yeast in mixing bowl and let stand 5 minutes. Stir.
- Add butter, sugar and salt.
- Gradually mix in flour.
- Beat thoroughly for 5 minutes, or 2 minutes with electric beater on slow speed.
- Add in additional flour to point where dough is just barely firm enough to handle.
- Knead on a well floured surface.
- Divide dough in 2 parts. Roll each into a 12″ circle.
- Butter each circle lightly and cut like a pie into 12 parts.
- Roll each section beginning with larger edge.
- Curve rolled roll, tucking in ends.
- Arrange on greased cookie sheets. Cover and let rise until double in size, approximately 1 hour.
- Bake for 12 to 20 minutes. Serve warm.

Preparation Note: If you have been out skiing all day, you won't have time to come home and whip these up. Make them the day before and warm them up. Or, use frozen bread.

Apple Crisp
(Serves 6, Oven 350°)

½ cup butter
½ cup oatmeal
½ cup flour

½ cup brown sugar
8 apples, peeled
cinnamon

- Cream butter; add oatmeal, flour and sugar. Mix until mixture is crumbly.
- Slice a layer of apples into a buttered casserole and sprinkle with crumb mixture. Repeat layers ending with a crumb layer.
- Sprinkle top with cinnamon.
- Bake for 40 minutes or until apples are cooked. Serve warm.

Serving Suggestion: It's even better when served with ice cream.

Mid-Day Energizers

Submarine Loaf
(Serves 4-6)

French loaf
2 tomatoes, sliced
1 cup coleslaw
ham or salami slices

1 medium onion, thinly sliced
cheese, thinly sliced (Swiss,
   Mozzarella, Colby)
mustard or mayonnaise

- Cut French loaf horizontally and scoop out some of bread in centre.
- Construct sandwich on bottom half of loaf, layering tomato slices, coleslaw, meat, onion rings and cheese.
- Spread top half with mustard or mayonnaise.
- Replace top half and cut into 4 to 6 servings.

Preparation Note: When taking this for lunch on the hills, wrap it tightly in Saran or foil and place in knapsack.

Slope Lunch
(Serves 4-6)

Skier's Quick and Easy Pâté (below)
carrot and celery sticks (below)
French bread

assorted cheeses
fresh orange sections
wine

Skier's Quick and Easy Pâté
(Serves 4-6)
½ lb. fine liver sausage
4 oz. cream cheese

2 green onions finely chopped

- Blend ingredients and press into a crock with a lid.

Preparation Note: Best prepared a day ahead.

Carrot and Celery Sticks
- Prepare sticks and place in a container of water.

Serving Suggestion: Spread a brightly coloured cloth on the snow and arrange lunch.

Cheesy-Mac Delight
(Serves 8-10, Oven 350°)

4 cups macaroni, cooked
¼ cup chopped onion
1 cup sliced olives
4 eggs, slightly beaten
1¼ cups light cream
1 tsp. seasoned salt

pepper
½ tsp. sugar
1 cup grated Parmesan
3 cups (12 ozs.) cheddar
2 tbsp. butter

- Combine cooked macaroni, onion, olives, egg, cream, salt, pepper and sugar.
- Add Parmesan and cheddar; toss all together.
- Butter a 12 cup bundt pan and lightly sprinkle with flour. Pour mixture into pan.
- Bake for 40 to 45 minutes.
- Cool 10 minutes; loosen edges and invert onto serving platter.

Georgian Cheese Bread
(Serves 8-10, Oven 375°)

The best way to describe this is a fondue in reverse. The coriander and cheese filling, a unique flavour in itself, is encased in a lovely light bread. This is nice served for brunch or a special lunch accompanied by your favourite salad, or as a late night lunch.

1 recipe Dough (below)

1 recipe Cheese Filling (below)

Dough

2 pkgs. active dry yeast
½ tsp. sugar
¼ tsp. ginger
1 cup lukewarm milk (110-115°)
3½-4 cups all purpose flour

½ cup cold milk
1 tbsp. sugar
2 tbsp. salt
½ cup softened butter

- Sprinkle yeast, ½ tsp. sugar and ginger into warm milk. Let stand 2 to 3 minutes; stir to dissolve. Place in a warm, draft-free location for 5 to 8 minutes, or until mixture doubles in size.
- Place 3½ cups flour in a large bowl. Make a deep well in the flour. Add ½ cup cold milk, yeast mixture, remaining sugar, salt and butter. Beat until smooth.
- Use remaining flour to flour kneading surface. Knead, adding flour as needed, for 10 minutes. Place in a buttered bowl, dust the dough with flour and cover with a clean cloth. Place in a warm, draft-free location and let rise 45 to 60 minutes until double in size.
- Punch down dough. Allow to rise a further 30 to 40 minutes until double in size.

Preparation Note: Frozen bread dough can also be used. Follow package directions.

Cheese Filling

2 lb. cheese — sweet Munster or Danish
  Elbo, finely grated
2 tbsp. butter

1 egg
1 tbsp. coriander, finely chopped

- Combine cheese with other ingredients. Beat until puréed.

Preparation Note: There is room to experiment here. You need 2 lbs. of cheese. Use one or the other, or a combination of both.

To Assemble:
- Lightly flour work surface and roll dough into a 22″ circle. Centre dough over a 9″ cake or flan pan. Place Cheese Filling in centre.
- Fold dough over cheese mixture in pleats. Bunch centre and twist into a knob.
- Let stand 15 minutes.
- Bake approximately 1 hour. Serve warm.

Egg Cheese Spread

½ lb. grated cheddar cheese
2 tbsp. minced onion
dash of cayenne pepper
¼ tsp. salt
1 hard cooked egg, chopped

1 tbsp. butter
1 tbsp. sugar
1 tbsp. flour
2 tbsp. vinegar
½ cup milk

- Mix grated cheese, onion, pepper and salt with chopped egg.
- Melt butter in a double boiler; add sugar and flour and blend well.
- To butter mixture, add vinegar and milk, stirring slowly and constantly. Cook over hot water until thickened.
- Combine with cheese mixture, and pour into sterilized jar. Store in refrigerator. Keeps for several weeks.

Serving Suggestion: This is an excellent spread for sandwiches or crackers and as a filling for celery sticks.

Meal-In-One Soups

Fish Soup
(Serves 4-6)

2 tbsp. butter
1½ tsp. garlic powder
1 large onion, chopped
½ cup chopped celery with leaves
2 16oz. cans tomatoes, cut up
¾ cup dry white wine

¼ cup minced parsley
2 tbsp. dill weed
1 tsp. salt
¼ tsp. pepper
1 pkg. (1 pound) frozen fish fillets, thawed

- In a large saucepan, melt butter and add garlic powder.
- Add onion and celery and cook until onions are clear and tender.
- Stir in tomatoes, wine, parsley, dill weed, salt and pepper. Simmer, covered, for 20 minutes.
- Cut fish fillets into 1" chunks. Add fish and simmer another 10 minutes or until fish flakes with a fork. Serve hot.

Pork Hocks and Lima Bean Soup
(Serves 6, Oven 350°)

2 cups dry lima beans
water to cover beans
4 ham hocks
2 bay leaves
1 large onion, chopped
1 green pepper, sliced in rounds

1 can (1 lb.) solid pack tomatoes
1 can (8 oz.) tomato sauce
1 tbsp. salt
pepper
¼ tsp. ground cloves

- Soak beans overnight in water.
- Without draining beans, add ham hocks, bay leaves and more water (if needed) to cover the beans. Simmer about 1 hour or until beans are tender.
- Add onion, green pepper, tomatoes, tomato sauce, salt, pepper and cloves. Mix until well blended and pour into a 4 quart casserole.
- Cover and bake for 1 hour or until meat is tender.
- Remove hocks from beans. Remove meat from bone and chop. Return meat to soup before serving.

Sauerkraut Soup

(Serves 6)

1 lb. spareribs or ham
½ lb. mushrooms
2 onions
1 can (14 oz.) tomatoes
1 jar (14 oz.) sauerkraut, drained and rinsed
1 small red cabbage, shredded
2 medium potatoes (optional)

1 cup tomato juice
1 clove garlic
salt and pepper
1 bay leaf
⅛ tsp. lemon juice

- Place meat in soup kettle and just cover with water. Simmer for 1 hour. Skim off fat. Remove ham. (If using spare ribs, leave in broth.)
- Fry mushrooms and onions and add to broth.
- Add tomatoes, sauerkraut, shredded cabbage, potatoes, tomato juice, garlic and spices. Simmer over low heat for 1½ hours.

Borsch

(Serves 10-12)

3-4 lbs. short ribs of beef
3 quarts water
½ cup red wine
4 tsp. salt
3 whole cloves
4 whole black peppercorns
1 bay leaf
4 large unpeeled beets, diced large

2 large carrots, cut in ¾" slices
2 stalks celery, cut in ½" slices
1 medium potato, diced large
2 large onions, diced large
1 16oz. can tomatoes
1 small head cabbage
2 tbsp. lemon juice
1 tbsp. sugar

- In large pan, place meat, water, wine and spices. Bring to a boil and simmer for 1 hour.
- Add beets and cook 1 more hour.
- Remove meat from broth and set aside.
- Add carrots, celery, potato, onion and tomatoes to broth.
- Cut meat from bones, discard fat and bone, and add meat to soup. Simmer 1 hour.
- Bring soup to boil. Cut cabbage into 1" wedges, remove core, and add cabbage to soup. Simmer 10 minutes.
- Stir in lemon juice and sugar just before serving.

Preparation Note: When preparing ahead, complete first 5 steps. 20 minutes before serving, complete the last 2 steps.

Serving Suggestion: A dollop of sour cream can be added to each bowl of soup at serving time.

Heart Warmers

Hot Toddy
(Serves 1)

1 tsp. sugar
jigger rum
4 oz. boiling water

1 twist of lemon or orange peel
cinnamon stick
3 cloves

Combine ingredients in a mug. Stir to dissolve sugar. Remove cloves.

Café Saronno
(Serves 1)

1 oz. rum
1 oz. Amaretto
4 oz. strong hot coffee

whipped cream
almond flakes

In a large cup, combine rum, Amaretto and coffee. Top with whipped cream and almonds.

Casino Royale
(Serves 1)

4 oz. strong hot coffee
1 jigger dark rum, warmed

1 scoop softened vanilla ice cream
nutmeg

Combine coffee and rum in a mug. Top with ice cream and sprinkle with nutmeg.

Hot Moo Juice

1 jigger crème de cacao
1 tsp. sugar

6 oz. hot milk
cinnamon

Combine liqueur and hot milk. Stir in sugar and sprinkle with cinnamon.

Chocolate Rum

6 oz. hot chocolate
1 jigger dark rum

whipped cream
chocolate chips

Combine hot chocolate and rum. Float whipped cream on top and dot with a couple of chocolate chips.

Fireside Coffee Nog
(Serves 10½ cups)

4 cups cold milk
3 tbsp. instant coffee
6 eggs
¾ cup sugar

1 cup light rum
½ pint whipping cream
1 pint coffee or vanilla ice cream

- Heat 1 cup of the milk and stir in coffee. Chill.
- Beat eggs until thick and lemon coloured. Gradually beat in sugar.
- Stir in coffee mixture, rum, and the remaining 3 cups of milk.
- Whip cream until softly stiff and fold into milk mixture.
- Mixture may be served in a punch bowl or in individual servings. Spoon ice cream on top of drink just before serving.

"It's Still Snowing . . . Why Don't You Stay For Dinner?"
Menu A: Cuisine Bourgeoise
Cream of Pea Soup
Tea Biscuits
Lettuce and Tomato Salad
Gougère with Ham and Mushrooms
Poires Belle Hélène

Cream of Pea Soup
(Serves 4)

2 tbsp. butter
¼ cup onions, finely chopped
1 clove garlic, crushed
1 tbsp. flour
2 cups Chicken Stock (see Basics, page 207)

3 cups frozen or fresh peas
½ cup whipping cream (canned evaporated milk may be substituted)
salt
2 tbsp. chopped parsley or chives

- In a saucepan, melt butter and add onions and garlic. Cook until soft, about 3 minutes.
- Stir in flour. Blend well.
- Add chicken stock. Bring to a boil, stirring constantly.
- Add peas and heat 5 minutes.
- Purée mixture in a blender.
- To serve, return to heat. Stir in cream. Add salt to taste. Top with parsley or chives.

Lettuce and Tomato Salad
(Serves 4-6)

5 cups romaine lettuce, chopped
12 cherry tomatoes

1 recipe Dressing (below)

- Place lettuce and tomatoes in a large salad bowl.
- Add Dressing and toss.

Dressing
½ cup vegetable oil
2 tbsp. lemon juice
dash of cayenne pepper

½ tsp. sugar
pepper

- Combine ingredients in a container with a lid and shake well.

Gougère with Ham and Mushrooms
(Serves 4-6, Oven 400°)

1 recipe Pâté à Choux

1 recipe Filling

Pâté à Choux

1 cup sifted flour
pinch of salt and pepper
1 cup water

½ cup butter or margarine
4 eggs
½ cup sharp cheddar cheese, diced

- Combine dry ingredients in a bowl or on a sheet of waxed paper.
- Heat water and butter in a large saucepan until butter melts. Increase heat and bring water to a boil.
- Add flour mixture all at once and stir vigorously until mixture forms a ball in centre of pan (approximately 1 minute). Cool mixture 5 minutes.
- Add eggs, one at a time, beating well with a wooden spoon after each addition.
- Stir in cheese. Blend well.

Filling

4 tbsp. butter or margarine
1 cup chopped onions
½ lb. sliced mushrooms, or, 1 10oz. can mushrooms, drained
1½ tbsp. flour
1 tsp. salt
¼ tsp. pepper

1 cup Chicken Broth (see Basics, page 207)
2 cups tomatoes, drained and chopped
6 oz. cooked ham (1½ cups), cut in thin strips
2 tbsp. shredded cheddar cheese
2 tbsp. parsley

- Melt butter in a large skillet; sauté onion until tender but not browned.
- Add mushrooms and continue cooking 2 minutes.
- Sprinkle with flour, salt and pepper; mix and cook an additional 2 minutes.
- Add broth and mix well. Bring to boiling, stirring constantly. Simmer 4 minutes. Remove from heat.
- Add tomatoes and ham.
- Butter a 10 to 11" oven proof skillet, pie plate, or shallow baking dish. Spoon the Pâté à Choux in a ring around the edge, leaving the centre open. Pour the Filling into the centre and sprinkle with cheese.
- Bake for 40 minutes or until Gougère is puffed and golden, and the filling is bubbling.
- Sprinkle with parsley and serve at once. Cut into wedges as for pie.

Poires Belle Hélène

(Serves 4)

1 pint vanilla ice cream
1 10oz. can pear halves

1 recipe Hot Chocolate Sauce (below)
¼ cup slivered almonds

- Place one scoop of ice cream in each dessert dish.
- Place half a pear on each serving and coat with Hot Chocolate Sauce.
- Sprinkle with almonds.

Hot Chocolate Sauce

2 squares unsweetened chocolate
½ cup light corn syrup
2 tbsp. sugar

¼ tsp. vanilla
½ tbsp. butter
½ cup evaporated milk

- Melt chocolate in corn syrup over low heat.
- Add sugar, vanilla and butter. Stir until butter is melted.
- Slowly add milk. Stir until well blended and serve at once.

"It's Still Snowing . . . Why Don't You Stay For Dinner?"

Menu B: Instant Class
Cheater Mushroom Soup
Cheese Bread
Crab Quiche
Basil Buttered Green Beans
Peaches Flambé

Cheater Mushroom Soup

(Serves 4)

1 can cream of mushroom soup
1 10oz. can sliced mushrooms, drained
½ cup white wine

¾ cup evaporated milk
nutmeg

- In a saucepan combine soup, mushrooms, wine, and milk. Heat.
- Sprinkle with nutmeg. Serve.

Cheese Bread

(Serves 4, Oven 350°)

1 egg
1½ cups milk

3¾ cups tea biscuit mix (See Basics, page 211)
1 cup sharp cheddar cheese, grated

- Beat egg and add milk.
- Stir in tea biscuit mix and cheese. Beat 30 seconds until well blended.
- Grease a 9″ x 5″ x 3″ loaf pan and line with waxed paper.
- Place batter in prepared pan and bake 1 hour.
- Let cool a few minutes before serving. Serve warm and cut in thick slices.

Crab Quiche
(Serves 4-6, Oven 350°)

1 10″ pie crust (see Basics, page 212)
1 7oz. can crabmeat, drained
½ cup Swiss cheese, grated
5 eggs, beaten

2½ cups cream or evaporated milk
¼ tsp. salt
⅛ tsp. pepper
dash nutmeg

- Spread crabmeat and cheese evenly over bottom of unbaked pie shell.
- Mix eggs, cream and seasonings. Pour over crab and cheese mixture.
- Bake 1 hour or until top is golden brown.

Preparation Note: If you do not have pastry prepared ahead and in the freezer, try this crumb crust:

2 cups cracker crumbs   6 tbsp. butter

- Place crumbs in a bowl.
- Melt butter and add to crumb mixture. Mix well.
- Spread crumb mixture in pie plate.
- Bake in 400° oven for 5 minutes.

Basil Buttered Green Beans
(Serves 4)

2 cups frozen or canned green beans   pinch of basil
3 tbsp. butter

- Heat beans and drain.
- Add butter and basil. Toss lightly. Serve.

Peaches Flambé
(Serves 4)

1 16oz. can peach halves
2 drops almond extract
2 drops vanilla extract

1½ tsp. cornstarch
dash of nutmeg and cinnamon
¼ cup brandy, rum, or orange flavoured
　　liqueur
vanilla ice cream

- Drain peaches, reserving syrup. Add water to peach syrup to equal 1½ cups of liquid.
- To liquid, add almond and vanilla extract, cornstarch, nutmeg and cinnamon. Place in a chafing dish. Heat mixture, stirring until blended and thickened.
- Add peach halves to liquid and heat. Do not boil.
- Warm liquor.
- Place chafing dish over heat at the table. Ignite liquor and pour flaming over fruit mixture. Allow flame to die down.
- Serve over vanilla ice cream.

"It's Still Snowing . . . Why Don't You Stay For Dinner?"
Menu C: Frost-Free Dinner
Sole Florentine
Oven Sautéed Carrots
Poppy Seed Bread Sticks
Beet and Orange Salad
Peachy Upside Down Cake

Sole Florentine
(Serves 4, Oven 350°)

1 lb. fresh or frozen spinach
salt and pepper
juice of one half lemon

1½ lbs. sole or haddock fillets
1 recipe Cheesy White Sauce (below)
Parmesan cheese

- Cook spinach and drain well.
- In a shallow greased baking dish, arrange spinach to cover bottom of dish. Sprinkle with salt, pepper and lemon juice.
- Place fillets of fish on bed of spinach.
- Pour Cheesy White Sauce over fish and sprinkle with Parmesan cheese.
- Bake in oven for 20 minutes or until fish flakes with a fork.

Cheesy White Sauce
(Yields 1 cup)

1 tbsp. butter
1 tbsp. flour
¾ cup milk or cream

1 tbsp. mayonnaise
1 tbsp. cheese spread

- Place butter and flour in saucepan. Blend over low heat until mixture is bubbling.
- Slowly blend in milk or cream and cook, stirring constantly, until thick.
- Add mayonnaise and cheese spread. Continue cooking until blended.

Oven Sautéed Carrots
(Serves 4, Oven 350°)

1 tbsp. butter
1 10½oz. can baby whole carrots

salt and pepper
2 tsp. grated Parmesan cheese

- In a shallow baking dish, melt butter.
- Drain carrots and place in dish, stirring to coat carrots with butter.
- Sprinkle with salt, pepper and Parmesan cheese.
- Bake 10 to 15 minutes in oven, stirring occasionally.

Poppy Seed Bread Sticks
(Yields 10-15, Oven 350°)

butter   poppy seeds
2-3 slices bread

- Butter both sides of bread generously and cut each slice into 5 strips.
- Place on a baking sheet. Sprinkle poppy seeds over bread sticks.
- Place in oven and bake until crisp, turning frequently (approximately 10 minutes).

Beet and Orange Salad
(Serves 4)

2 large oranges   1 10oz. can sliced beets, drained
2 bunches watercress or torn lettuce   1 recipe Tarragon Dressing (below)

- Grind rind of 1 orange and set aside. (for Tarragon Dressing)
- Peel both oranges and remove white pith. Slice into rounds.
- Arrange watercress or lettuce on a shallow serving dish.
- Overlap slices of beets and oranges in alternate layers on bed of greens.
- Spoon Tarragon Dressing over layers just before serving.

Tarragon Dressing

4 tbsp. oil   ¼ tsp. tarragon
1½ tbsp. wine vinegar   ½ tsp. salt
1 tsp. prepared mustard   ½ tsp. sugar

- Blend all ingredients and add reserved orange rind. Mix well.

Peachy Upside Down Cake
(Serves 6-8, Oven 350°)

3 tbsp. butter   8 maraschino cherries
¼ cup brown sugar   1 recipe White Cake (see Basics, page 208)
3-4 cups peach halves or slices, drained

- In a 9″ square pan, melt butter over low heat.
- Remove from heat; sprinkle brown sugar over bottom of pan.
- Arrange peaches in pan with cherries.
- Pour cake batter slowly over fruit. Bake for 40 to 45 minutes.
- Remove from oven and immediately invert on serving dish. Let stand 10 minutes before removing cake pan. Serve warm.

Serving Suggestion: Top with whipped or ice cream.

Valentine's Day

Breakfast in Bed
Dinner à Deux
Midnight Sonata

Chapter Six: Valentine's Day: Two's Company
Breakfast in Bed
Dinner à Deux
Midnight Sonata

Valentine's Day:
Two's Company

February in Huronia brings crisp wintry days, sudden snows, and Valentines.

Now is the time for those special heart-warming dinners at the fireside with delicate wines and delectable foods. Our "Two's Company" chapter is simple but luxurious, with foods guaranteed to create the feeling of love and romance. Try an enchanting midnight supper, or a romantic breakfast in bed. Bring together our dining ideas with two people in love . . . and don't forget the champagne.

Breakfast in Bed
(For 2)

Sunrise Cocktail
Crêpe D'Amour
Amber Marmalade
Muffins
(More Champagne)
(Coffee)

Sunrise Cocktail

champagne   orange juice

- Mix equal parts chilled champagne and orange juice.
- Pour into large frosted wine goblets.

Preparation Note: To frost glasses, place in freezer for at least one hour.

Crêpe D'Amour
(Serves 2, Oven 350°)

1 recipe Crêpe   1 recipe Filling

Crêpe
2 eggs, beaten   ½ cup milk
½ tsp. salt   4 tbsp. butter, melted
¼ cup flour   2 tbsp. butter to grease pan

- Combine eggs, salt, flour, milk and butter until smooth.
- Place 2 tbsp. butter in an 8" glass pie plate. Place in oven and warm till bubbly. Remove.
- Pour batter mixture over melted butter; return to oven and bake 25 minutes.
- Prepare Filling (below).
- Remove Crêpe from oven; loosen from pie plate. Place Filling on one half of the Crêpe and fold over. Secure with a toothpick and sprinkle top with grated cheddar cheese.
- Place filled Crêpe under broiler until cheese has melted (approximately 3 minutes). Cut in half and serve.

Filling
¼ cup chopped mushrooms   2 tbsp. butter
¼ cup chopped onions   ½ cup grated cheddar cheese
¼ cup chopped green peppers

- Sauté mushrooms, onions and peppers in butter. Set aside.
- Reserve grated cheddar cheese for topping.

Preparation Note: Crêpe will puff up during cooking, but will fall when removed from the oven.

130

Amber Marmalade
(Yields six 8 oz. jars)

1 grapefruit   2 oranges
1 lemon   7 cups sugar

- Wash fruit and thinly slice, discarding end pieces and seeds.
- Quarter grapefruit slices; cut orange and lemon slices in half.
- Measure fruit and place in a heavy pot. Add 1 cup of water for each cup of fruit.
- Cover and let fruit stand in a cool place for 12 hours or overnight.
- Bring fruit to a boil, stirring frequently until peel is tender, (approximately 40 minutes).
- Measure fruit and cooking liquid and add 1 cup of sugar for each cup of combined fruit and liquid. Stir to dissolve sugar.
- Return to stove and boil, stirring frequently, until marmalade reaches the gel stage (approximately 30 minutes). (Watch carefully as marmalade scorches easily.)
- Pour hot marmalade into sterilized jars and seal immediately.

Preparation Note: This marmalade can be made anytime of the year.

Muffins
(Yields 6 muffins, Oven 400°)

½ recipe Tea Biscuit Mix — Muffins,   ¼ cup marmalade
   omitting fruit (see Basics, page 211)

- Combine ingredients for Muffins with marmalade.
- Fill greased muffin tins and bake 20 to 25 minutes.

Dinner à Deux
St. Valentine
Cold Cucumber Soup
Shrimp and Crabmeat Madeira
Bibb and Endive Salad
(Champagne)
Café Royale

St. Valentine
(Serves 2)

1 tsp. sugar   6 oz. chilled champagne
1½ oz. brandy

- Dissolve sugar in brandy.
- Add champagne and crushed ice.
- Stir gently and strain off the ice.
- Divide drink between two wine goblets. Serve.

Cold Cucumber Soup
(Serves 2)

1 medium cucumber, unpeeled   1 tsp. dill
1 cup Chicken Broth (see Basics,   salt and pepper to taste
  page 207)   chives for garnish
1 cup yoghurt

- Combine all ingredients in blender and purée.
- Chill well before serving and garnish with chopped chives.

Shrimp and Crabmeat Madeira
(Serves 2)

3 tbsp. butter   1 tbsp. lemon juice
2 tbsp. chopped shallots   2 tsp. tomato paste
¾ cup sliced mushrooms   2 egg yolks
½ lb. uncooked shrimp   ¾ cup whipping cream
6 oz. cooked crab, drained   salt and pepper
½ cup Madeira   ½ lb. linguini
¼ tsp. tarragon   2 tbsp. chopped parsley

- Melt butter in saucepan. Add shallots and sauté until soft. Add mushrooms and sauté until liquid evaporates.
- Add shrimp and cook until they begin to turn pink. Add crab and stir in Madeira; cook

until liquid is almost completely reduced. Add tarragon, lemon juice and tomato paste. Mix thoroughly.
- Combine yolks with cream and very slowly add to saucepan, mixing constantly. Add salt and pepper to taste.
- Cook linguini according to package directions.
- Heat shrimp and crabmeat mixture thoroughly and serve on a bed of linguini. Top with chopped parsley.

Bibb and Endive Salad
(Serves 2)

1 head bibb lettuce
Belgian endive

1 recipe Sherry-Wine French Dressing (below)

- Rinse bibb lettuce and pat dry with paper towels.
- Halve and arrange each on a salad plate with 3 or 4 leaves of Belgian endive.
- Sprinkle ⅓ cup of Sherry-Wine French Dressing over each salad.

Sherry-Wine French Dressing
(Yields ⅔ cup)

1 tbsp. sherry
2 tbsp. wine vinegar
½ tsp. Dijon mustard

½ tsp. parsley
salt and pepper to taste
½ cup olive oil

- In a bowl combine first five ingredients.
- Add olive oil in a slow stream, whisking continuously.

Café Royale
(Serves 2)

1 cup strong coffee
2 sugar cubes

2 oz. warmed brandy

- Fill each demi-tasse half full with coffee and add a sugar cube.
- Add 1 oz. of brandy, pouring brandy off the back of a spoon. (This way the brandy floats on top of the coffee.)
- Ignite brandy. Pour more coffee over flaming brandy.

Serving Suggestion: A nice finale to this dinner is Brie and Roquefort cheese, water biscuits, green grapes, fresh pears and more Café Royale.

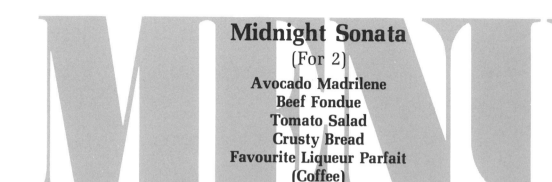

Midnight Sonata
(For 2)
Avocado Madrilene
Beef Fondue
Tomato Salad
Crusty Bread
Favourite Liqueur Parfait
(Coffee)
(Champagne)

Avocado Madrilène
(Serves 2)

1 avocado
lemon juice
¼ cup diced cucumber

½ cup Jellied Consommé (see Basics,
   page 208)
2 tbsp. sour cream
chives

- Cut avocado in half; do not peel. Twist gently to remove pit. Sprinkle exposed surface with lemon juice to keep avocado from darkening.
- Spoon cucumber on avocado. Spoon Jellied Consommé over cucumber.
- Chill until ready to serve. To serve, top with a dollop of sour cream and sprinkle with chives.

Beef Fondue
(Serves 2)

½ lb. butter
⅔ cup olive oil

1½ lbs. tender fillet of beef cut into ¾" cubes
Sauces (below)

- Melt butter in a fondue pot; add olive oil and bring mixture to a boil. Place fondue pot over flame, adjusting heat to keep the oil and butter bubbling hot during the cooking process.
- Spear cubes of beef and cook to desired taste in oil and butter mixture. Dip in Sauces.

Sauces

Tomato Sauce
(Yields 1½ cups)

1 cup chili sauce
¼ cup brown sugar
¼ cup water

2 tbsp. Worcestershire sauce
2 tbsp. prepared mustard

- Combine all ingredients in a saucepan; blend well. Cook over low heat stirring until hot. Can be served hot or chilled.

Garlic Sauce
(Yields 1¼ cups)

4 large garlic cloves, peeled
2 egg yolks
1 cup olive oil

1 tsp. lemon juice
¼ tsp. pepper

- Mash garlic. Place garlic and egg yolks in a blender and blend well.
- Add olive oil in a stream, processing all the while. Process until it is the consistency of mayonnaise.
- Stir in remaining ingredients and chill.

Horseradish Sauce
(Yields 1½ cups)

½ cup ketchup
½ cup mayonnaise

1 tbsp. Worcestershire sauce
5 tbsp. prepared horseradish

- Mix all ingredients together and chill.

Curry Sauce
(Yields 1½ cups)

1 cup mayonnaise
6 tsp. curry powder

3 tbsp. milk

- Place all ingredients in blender. Cover and blend at low speed. Refrigerate until ready to use.

Tomato Salad
(Serves 2)

4 tomatoes, cut in wedges
½ cup onion, chopped

1 recipe Dressing (below)

- Combine Dressing ingredients in a container with a lid. Shake well.
- Drizzle over tomatoes and onion. Chill before serving.

Dressing
½ cup vinegar
½ cup oil

1 tsp. Dijon mustard
1 tbsp. sugar

Crusty Bread
(Yields 2 loaves, Oven 400°)

½ the recipe for White Bread (see Basics, page 210)
corn meal

- Prepare bread and allow to rise twice.
- Divide dough in two.
- On a floured surface, roll out dough into a rectangle 10″ wide and 14″ long. Roll up width and pinch ends.
- Grease cookie sheet and sprinkle lightly with corn meal. Place bread rolled up on cookie sheet.
- Brush with cold water. Place a pan of hot water on lower oven rack. Bake approximately 35 minutes to a nice golden brown. Brush with cold water twice more during baking.

Preparation Note: Water is to make bread nice and crusty. Instead of brushing bread with water during baking, you can use a spritzer bottle and spray water in oven during baking.

Favourite Liqueur Parfait

ice cream   favourite liqueur

- Alternate ice cream and your favourite liqueur in parfait glasses.

Winterama

Warm-up Dinner
Carnival Lunch
Ever-Ready Carnival Supper
"They're Coming for the Weekend":
—Friday Night Winter Picnic
—Saturday Lunch
—Saturday Dinner
—Sunday Brunch

Chapter Seven: Winterama

Warm-up Dinner
Carnival Lunch
Ever-Ready Carnival Supper
"They're Coming for the Weekend":
—Friday Night Winter Picnic
—Saturday Lunch
—Saturday Dinner
—Sunday Brunch

Winterama

Winter carnivals can be fun for the whole family. In the southern Georgian Bay region, carnival time runs from mid January to the end of February. A carnival weekend offers lots of spectator and participatory events, and of course, lots of good eating.

Barrie boasts a Winter Carnival in February, Wasaga Beach has a Winter Jamboree in January, and, in Collingwood, a Winterfest is held in February along with the Winter Carnival in Orillia.

The oldest winter carnival takes place in Penetanguishene, usually during the last weekend in February. Historically, it marks the wedding celebration of Kitchekewana, the legendary giant Huron Indian who lived here many years ago and protected the local tribes. Legend has it that Kitchekewana now lies at rest in Giants Tomb, the beautiful island in southern Georgian Bay.

One of the newcomers to the winter carnival scene is the Mini Bonhomme Carnival held in Victoria Harbour. During this February weekend, one might see the Winter Olympics with participants from local public schools, a snowmobile torchlight parade, a cross country ski race, sky divers, and much more. For more information on carnivals and other winter activities, we suggest that you pick up a copy of "This is Ontario— Winter", distributed free at Brewer's Retail Stores throughout Ontario.

Carnival time is a fun-filled celebration of winter and everything it has to offer to those of us in the rural areas of Ontario. Any celebration deserves good food, so why not try some of our Winterama menus to add to this happy time of year.

MENU

Warm-up Dinner
(For 10)
Baked Beans
Cabbage Raisin Salad
Oatmeal Bread
(Cheddar Cheese)
Apple Dumplings

Baked Beans
(Serves 10, Oven 325°)

4 cups dried white beans
12 cups cold water
2 cloves garlic
2 tsp. thyme
1 bay leaf
⅛ tsp. allspice
1 lb. sliced salt pork
2 onions

1 4oz. can tomato paste
1 cup brown sugar, lightly packed
1 tsp. dried mustard
½ cup butter, creamed
½ cup brown sugar
4 apples, cored and sliced
½ cup rum

- Wash beans and place in large kettle. Cover with cold water and soak overnight.
- Next day, add garlic, thyme, bay leaf and allspice to beans. Bring to a boil and simmer 1 hour.
- Remove bay leaf and garlic; discard.
- Line bean pot with sliced pork.
- To beans, add onions, tomato paste, 1 cup brown sugar and mustard. Mix.
- Pour into lined bean pot. Bake 4 to 5 hours.
- Cream butter and ½ cup brown sugar.
- During the last hour of cooking, cover beans with a layer of sliced apples. Top apples with butter and brown sugar mixture and pour rum over all. Return to oven and continue cooking.

Cabbage Raisin Salad
(Serves 10)

1 medium cabbage, shredded
1 small onion, chopped

1 cup raisins
1 cup mayonnaise

- Combine ingredients and toss until moistened. (You may need more mayonnaise.) Serve chilled.

Oatmeal Bread
(Yields 2 loaves, Oven 400°)

2 cups boiling water
2 cups rolled oats
½ cup molasses
1 tbsp. salt
½ cup brown sugar

½ cup shortening
2 packets of yeast
½ cup lukewarm water
1 tsp. sugar
6 cups flour

- In a large bowl, combine boiling water and oats. Stir and add molasses, salt, brown sugar and shortening. Stir until shortening has melted. Set aside until lukewarm.
- In a small bowl, dissolve yeast in lukewarm water and sugar.
- Add yeast to oat mixture.
- Gradually add flour, one cup at a time, mixing well after each addition. Continue adding flour in this fashion until dough clings together and is moist and easy to handle.
- Turn dough out onto a well floured surface and knead approximately 10 minutes, or until dough is smooth and elastic.
- Place dough in greased bowl. Cover bowl with waxed paper.
- Place bowl in warm, draft free place. Let rise 1 to 2 hours until double in size. Punch down.
- Divide dough in two and shape into loaves. Place in lightly greased loaf pans. Cover and let rise until double, approximately 1 hour.
- Bake 35 minutes.

Serving Suggestion: Serve a nice wedge of cheddar cheese along with salad, beans and bread.

Apple Dumplings
(Serves 10, Oven 350°)

2 cups flour
4 tsp. baking powder
1 tsp. salt
4 tbsp. shortening
1 cup milk

5 apples, pared, cored and cut in half
sugar
cinnamon
1 recipe Brown Sugar Sauce (below)

- Sift dry ingredients and cut in shortening.
- Add milk. Mix to a smooth dough.
- Turn onto a floured board, divide into 10 portions and roll each portion large enough to cover one half apple.
- Place half an apple on each piece of dough. Fill core hollow with sugar and cinnamon.
- Wet edges of dough and press together over apple.
- Place dumplings in casserole dish or baking dish.
- Pour Brown Sugar Sauce over dumplings.
- Bake 45 minutes. Serve warm.

Brown Sugar Sauce
1 cup water
2 cups brown sugar

3 tbsp. butter

- Combine ingredients in a saucepan and heat.

MENU

Carnival Lunch
(For 8)
Cranberry Cheer
Pea Soup
Open Faced Grilled Cheese and Onion Sandwich
Thick Cream Peach Pie

Cranberry Cheer
(Yields 6 cups)

1 quart cranberry juice
2¼ cups pineapple juice

1 tsp. whole cloves
4 sticks cinnamon

- Place ingredients in saucepan and bring to a boil.
- Remove from heat and serve at once.

Serving Suggestion: Rum is a nice added touch for adults.

Pea Soup
(Serves 8)

4 pork hocks
1 bay leaf
3 quarts water
1 lb. green split peas

3 carrots, sliced
3 onions, quartered
½ tsp. basil

- Place pork hocks and bay leaf in cold water. Bring to a boil and simmer 2 hours or until meat falls from the hocks.
- Strain broth. Place liquid in soup kettle; skim off fat. Reserve meat and allow to cool.
- Add split peas to skimmed broth. Bring to a boil, stirring constantly. Reduce heat and simmer 2 to 3 hours. Stir occasionally to prevent sticking to bottom. (Peas will purée on their own and thicken soup.)
- During last hour of cooking, add carrots, onions, basil and cooked meat.

Open Faced Grilled Cheese and Onion Sandwich
(Yields 1 sandwich)

1 slice buttered pumpernickel bread
1 oz. freshly grated Parmesan cheese

1 thin slice Spanish onion

- Sprinkle grated Parmesan evenly over buttered bread and top with sliced onion.
- Place 6 inches under the broiler and broil until the cheese is bubbly. Serve hot with soup.

Thick Cream Peach Pie
(Serves 8, Oven 425°)

pastry for 9" one crust pie
  (see Basics, page 212)
7 to 8 peaches, peeled and halved

2 eggs
1 cup sugar
1 cup sour cream

- Place peach halves in unbaked pie shell.
- Beat eggs and add sugar and sour cream; mix well.
- Pour mixture over peaches.
- Bake pie at 425° for 15 minutes, then reduce heat to 350° and bake another 35 minutes.

Ever-Ready Carnival Supper
(For 6)

**Mulled Wine
Pizza
Orange and Onion Salad
Gingerbread**

Mulled Wine
(Serves 6)

1 quart orange juice
½ cup white sugar
½ cup brown sugar
½ stick cinnamon

6 whole cloves
6 whole allspice
1 bottle port

- Mix orange juice and sugars in large saucepan.
- Tie spices in cheese cloth and add to orange juice. Heat and simmer 5 minutes.
- Add port and heat until just hot.

Pizza
(Yields 2 large pizzas, Oven 475°)

Dough (for 2 large pans)
1 pkg. yeast
1¼ cup warm water
3 cups flour

1 tsp. salt
1 tbsp. oil
1 recipe Topping (see next page)

- Dissolve yeast in warm water.
- Add 1 cup of the flour, salt and oil. Mix well.
- Add another 2 cups flour gradually and knead 15 minutes. Dough should be smooth and elastic.
- Shape into a round ball, and brush with oil. Let rise 3 hours in a warm place.
- Punch dough down and divide in two. Use right away or freeze separately in plastic wrap. To use after freezing, thaw completely and roll out.

143

Topping (for 2 large pizzas)

8 oz. tomato sauce
¼ tsp. oregano
2 cloves garlic, crushed
salt to taste
¼ cup chopped green onions

2 10½ oz. cans mushroom pieces, drained
2 green peppers, chopped
½ lb. pepperoni, sliced
8 oz. Mozzarella cheese, grated

- Divide tomato sauce evenly between the two pizza crusts.
- Sprinkle oregano over each.
- Top the sauce with crushed garlic, salt, chopped onion, mushroom pieces, green pepper, pepperoni and cheese.
- Bake for 20 to 25 minutes or until the crust is well done.

Serving Suggestion: Add any of your favourite ingredients such as olives, tomato slices, anchovies, etc.

Orange and Onion Salad
(Serves 6)

6 oranges
2 red onions

3 cups shredded lettuce
1 recipe French Dressing (below)

- Peel onions and oranges and slice thin.
- Shred lettuce.
- Combine and toss with French Dressing.

French Dressing
(Yields 1½ cups)

¼ cup wine vinegar
1 tsp. salt
⅛ tsp. pepper

½ tsp. sugar
½ tsp. dry mustard
1 cup oil

- Place all ingredients in a jar. Cover and shake well.

Gingerbread
(Serves 6-8, Oven 350°)

½ cup shortening, softened
½ cup sugar
1 egg
½ cup molasses
1½ cups flour

¾ tsp. salt
¾ tsp. soda
½ tsp. ginger
½ tsp. cinnamon
½ cup boiling water

- Cream shortening and gradually add sugar.
- Add eggs and molasses and beat thoroughly.
- Sift together dry ingredients; add to molasses mixture alternately with boiling water. Beat after each addition.
- Bake in greased 8″ x 8″ x 2″ pan for 35 to 40 minutes. Serve warm.

Serving Suggestion: Nice topped with whipped cream or vanilla ice cream.

"They're Coming for the Weekend"
Friday Night Winter Picnic
Saturday Lunch
Saturday Dinner
Sunday Brunch

Friday Night Winter Picnic
(For 8)
Salad Bar
Sandwich Creations
(Beer)
Lemon Cup
Spiced Tea

Friday Night Winter Picnic

As your guests arrive Friday evening, let them unwind with a relaxed winter picnic. All the ingredients can be prepared ahead of time. Set the salad bar up on the coffee table in the living room or on a summery cloth laid out in the centre of the room on the floor. The sandwich fixings can be laid out in the kitchen. Attach instructions for sandwich creations to the cupboard door; turn the oven on and sit back while everyone concocts their own dinner.

Salad Bar
(Serves 8)

9 cups mixed greens tossed in a salad bowl (Iceberg and romaine lettuce and spinach).

Side Dishes of:

tomato wedges	bacon bits
cucumber	chick peas
green and/or black olives	croutons
sliced Spanish onions	watercress
Parmesan cheese	chopped green pepper

Dressings

Anchovy Salad Dressing

½ cup salad oil   ¼ tsp. pepper
¼ cup vinegar   1 can (2 oz.) anchovy fillets, drained
1 tsp. salt   1 egg
dash of garlic powder

- Place all ingredients in blender container. Cover and process a few seconds until smooth. Chill before serving.

Dieter's Tangy Dressing

1 tbsp. corn starch   1 tsp. Worcestershire sauce
1½ tsp. sugar or sugar substitute ½ tsp. salt
1 tsp. dry mustard   ½ tsp. pepper
1 cup cold water   ½ tsp. paprika
¼ cup vinegar   dash of hot pepper sauce
¼ cup ketchup   1 clove garlic
1 tsp. lemon or lime juice
1 tsp. prepared horseradish

- In a saucepan, combine corn starch, sugar and dry mustard; gradually stir in cold water. Cook and stir over medium heat until thickened.
- Remove from heat and cool for 15 minutes.
- Place cooled mixture with remaining ingredients, excluding garlic, in blender and process for a few seconds.
- Pour into a jar and add garlic.
- Cover and chill. Remove garlic before serving.

Thousand Island Dressing

1¼ cups mayonnaise (see Basics,   3 peaches, quartered
  page 206)   2 tbsp. chopped green pepper
½ cup milk or light cream   1 tsp. lemon juice
⅓ cup chili sauce   2 hard cooked eggs
2 tbsp. chopped onion

- Place all ingredients, except eggs, in blender and process until vegetables and fruit are chopped. Scrape sides of blender with spatula.
- Slowly add eggs and process until eggs are coarsely chopped.
- Refrigerate until ready to serve.

Serving Suggestion: Have a cruet each of oil and vinegar, and lemon wedges on hand for the purest of salad lovers.

Sandwich Creations
(Serves 8, Oven 375°)

These are sandwiches concocted from a variety of meats, cheeses and shredded vegetables placed in bread dough and baked on the spot.

Basic White Bread Recipe (see Basics, page 210)
Whole Wheat Bread (see Basics, page 210)

These breads can be made up ahead of time and refrigerated for up to 24 hours. When ready to use, remove from refrigerator 20 minutes ahead of time. Uncover and let stand. Frozen commercial bread dough may also be used. Follow defrosting instructions on package.

Suggested Meat, Cheese and Fish Fillings
1 lb. medium ground beef, browned
1 cup diced, cooked ham
1 lb. Italian sausage
8 oz. pepperoni, cubed

8 oz. frozen or canned shrimp
1 7oz. can tuna, drained
3 oz. grated Mozzarella cheese
3 oz. grated old cheddar cheese

Vegetable Fillings
½ cup chopped onions
½ cup chopped green peppers
½ cup chopped mushrooms
¼ cup sliced olives

½ cup grated carrots
½ cup shredded zucchini
1 cup shredded cabbage

Herbs and Spices
salt
pepper
marjoram
rosemary

Condiments
mayonnaise
tangy mustard
prepared horseradish
butter

Set out ingredients in separate dishes, in an accessible spot in kitchen. Place greased cookie sheets or cake pans on top of stove. Position bread boards to work on, or an oil cloth also makes a good working area.

Post the following instructions:

To Make Sandwiches:
1. Pinch off a piece of dough a little larger than a golf ball.
2. Flour your working surface.
3. Pat out dough to a 5 or 6 inch circle.
4. Select desired filling combination to equal about ⅓ of a cup.
5. Place filling on half circle.
6. Fold over and seal dough with edge of fork.
7. Prick your initial on top.
8. Cover and let rest for 20 minutes.
9. Bake 18 to 20 minutes.
10. Brush with butter.
11. Enjoy

P.S. Help yourself to the beer while you are in the kitchen.

Lemon Cup
(Serves 8)

1 10-12oz. can pitted Bing cherries   1 recipe Lemon Sherbet (below)
6 oz. vodka   1 cup whipping cream, whipped

- Marinate cherries in vodka for at least one hour. Prepare Lemon Sherbet (below).
- Place Lemon Sherbet in sherbet glasses.
- Spoon marinated cherries over sherbet servings, reserving 8 cherries for the top of each dessert.
- Top each serving with whipped cream.
- Garnish with cherry.

Lemon Sherbet

4 tsp. unflavoured gelatin   1½ cups lemon juice
½ cup cold water   2 tsp. grated lemon rind
1½ cups sugar   ¼ tsp. salt
4½ cups water   4 egg whites, stiffly beaten

- Soak gelatin in ½ cup cold water for 5 minutes
- Combine sugar and 4½ cups water in saucepan and boil for 10 minutes.
- Dissolve gelatin mixture in hot syrup. Cool.
- Add lemon juice, rind and salt to syrup mixture.
- Fold in egg whites.
- Place in metal pan and cover with foil. Place in freezer. Freeze until slushy. Stir or beat 4 or 5 times at half hour intervals, working from front to back, to reduce the size of the crystals.
- Remove from freezer approximately 30 minutes before serving.

Spiced Tea
(Serves 8, Oven 300°)

½ cup loose orange pekoe tea   ½ tsp. finely chopped candied ginger
1 tbsp. finely shredded orange peel   ¼ tsp. whole cloves, coarsely crushed
¾″ stick cinnamon, coarsely grated

- Combine all ingredients in oven proof pan with a lid.
- Cover and heat in oven for 20 minutes.
- Place in a jar with a tight fitting lid. Seal. Store in a cool place for at least one week.
- To prepare tea, use 3 tsp. of mixture to 8 cups of boiling water. Steep 2 to 3 minutes.

MENU

Saturday Lunch
(For 8)

Spinach Soup
Welsh Rarebit
Sprout Salad
Fruit Bars

Spinach Soup
(Serves 8)

2 lb. fresh spinach, steamed
2 10oz. cans mushroom soup

3 cans milk or cream
nutmeg

- Blend spinach, soup and milk.
- Heat and serve sprinkled with nutmeg.

Welsh Rarebit
(Serves 8)

2 oz. butter
1 lb. cheddar cheese, grated
¾ cup milk
few drops Worcestershire sauce

2 tsp. prepared mustard
salt and pepper
8 slices bread

- Place butter, cheese, milk, Worcestershire sauce, mustard, salt and pepper in a saucepan.
- Heat stirring constantly until sauce is thick and smooth.
- Toast bread.
- Pour mixture over bread and return to broiler to brown. Serve hot.

Serving Suggestion: For a different flavour, use beer instead of milk.

Sprout Salad
(Serves 8)

2 cucumbers, thinly sliced
6 tomatoes, thinly sliced
1 recipe Spice Dressing (see next page)

salad greens
2 cups alfalfa sprouts
dill weed

- Place cucumber and tomato slices alternately in a shallow dish.
- Pour Dressing over and allow to marinate in refrigerator for an hour.
- Garnish the outside edges of the dish with salad greens and fill in with a light layer of sprouts.
- Sprinkle dill weed over sprouts. Chill and serve.

Spice Dressing

(Yields 1¼ cups)

½ tsp. garlic powder
¼ tsp. dry mustard
⅛ tsp. pepper
1 tsp. salt
¼ tsp. paprika

2 tsp. sugar
¾ cup oil
¼ cup vinegar
2 tbsp. tomato juice

• Combine ingredients and chill.

Fruit Bars

(Yields 8″ cake, Oven 350°)

⅔ cup flour
1 tsp. baking powder
½ tsp. salt
1 cup walnuts
¾ cup dates or raisins
¾ cup candied fruit

2 eggs
⅔ cup sugar
⅓ cup corn oil
1 tsp. vanilla
1 recipe Lemon Glaze (below)

• Mix dry ingredients together.
• Stir in nuts and fruit.
• Beat eggs, sugar, corn oil and vanilla and add to dry ingredients. Blend well.
• Place in a well greased 8″ cake pan and bake for 40 minutes.
• Cool and top with Lemon Glaze.
• Slice into bars.

Lemon Glaze

1½ tsp. oil
1 tbsp. lemon juice

½ tsp. lemon rind
1 cup icing sugar

• Combine oil, juice and rind and heat.
• Stir in icing sugar and blend.
• While still warm, drizzle over squares.

MENU

Saturday Dinner

(For 8)

Parsley Soup
Chicken with Dumplings
Pineapple Jellied Salad
Fried Zucchini
Porridge Apples

Parsley Soup

(Serves 8)

1 medium onion, chopped
¼ lb. butter
3 cups Chicken Stock (see Basics, page 207)
⅛ tsp. dry mustard

1 pint half and half cream
1 large bunch fresh parsley leaves
salt and pepper to taste

- In a large skillet sauté onions in butter.
- Add stock and dry mustard. Stir and remove from heat.
- Add cream and parsley. Season with salt and pepper.
- Purée until smooth.
- Chill 1 to 2 hours. Serve cold.

Chicken with Dumplings

(Serves 8)

1 5lb. chicken, cut into pieces
5 cups water
2 bay leaves
1 tsp. poultry seasoning
3-4 peppercorns

5 carrots, cut in pieces
6 small onions, quartered
5 stalks celery, cut in pieces
1 recipe Dumplings (see next page)
2 tbsp. corn starch

- Simmer chicken in water for 15 minutes, spooning off froth.
- Continue to simmer for 45 minutes.
- Add bay leaves, poultry seasoning, peppercorns and continue to simmer for 1 hour.
- Remove meat from pot and strain. Reserve chicken.
- Return stock to pot. Add carrots, onions, celery and cook until vegetables are tender, approximately 45 minutes.
- Remove chicken from bones. Discard bones and skin and return meat to pot. Prepare Dumplings (below).
- Drop Dumplings by spoonful into stock. Cover and cook 20 minutes over medium heat.
- When Dumplings are cooked, thicken stock with corn starch.

Dumplings

2 cups flour
1 tsp. salt
4 tsp. baking powder
½ tsp. pepper
1 tsp. sage

1 tsp. savory
1 egg, well beaten
3 tbsp. melted butter
1 cup milk

- Sift dry ingredients.
- Add egg, butter, and milk; stir. Batter will be moist and stiff.

Fried Zucchini
(Serves 8)

8 small zucchini
¼ cup butter or margarine
½ tsp. garlic powder

½ tsp. salt
⅛ tsp. pepper

- Slice each zucchini in half, lengthwise.
- Melt butter in large frying pan and add garlic, salt and pepper.
- Over medium heat, cook and roll zucchini in butter mixture until slightly brown.
- Cover and cook 5 to 8 minutes further or until zucchini is crisp and tender.

Pineapple Jellied Salad
(Serves 8)

1 6oz. pkg. pineapple jello
1 14oz. can crushed pineapple

½ cup pecans
1 large apple

- Make jello according to package instructions and chill until partially set.
- Drain pineapple, chop pecans and dice apple.
- Fold all three into jello and chill.

Porridge Apples
(Serves 8, Oven 350°)

2 cups rolled oats
1 cup brown sugar, lightly packed
¼ tsp. salt
1 cup butter

8 medium cooking apples, peeled, cored
  and thinly sliced
2½ cups water
1 large apple, cored and thinly sliced
2 tbsp. honey, warmed

- Grease a large baking dish and set aside.
- In a medium sized bowl, combine the oats, sugar, salt and butter, stirring well with a wooden spoon to blend.
- Layer the oat mixture and apple slices in the prepared dish, beginning and ending with a layer of oat mixture.
- Carefully pour the water over the mixture.
- Place the unpeeled apple slices decoratively over the top of the pudding and using a pastry brush, brush them with honey.
- Cook in oven 40 to 50 minutes until pudding is deep golden brown. Serve warm.

MENU

Sunday Brunch
(For 8)
Tarte au Poisson
Tossed Salad with Paprika Dressing
Honeydew Melon
Poppy Swirl

Tarte au Poisson
(Serves 4-6, Oven 350°)

pastry for 9″ single pie crust (see Basics, page 212)
1 lb. fish fillets (thawed)
½ cup dry white wine
1 tsp. salt
dash of pepper
½ bay leaf
1 medium onion, sliced
1½ cups water
2 tbsp. butter
2 tbsp. flour
1 cup sour cream
lemon slices
chopped parsley

- Prepare a 9″ single pie crust.
- In a large skillet, combine fish with wine, salt, pepper, bay leaf, onion and water.
- Cook, covered, over low heat for 15 minutes or until fish flakes easily when tested with a fork.
- Drain fish reserving ⅔ cup of liquid and cooked onion. Flake fish and set aside.
- Slowly melt butter in medium saucepan. Remove from heat. Stir in flour to make a smooth mixture.
- Gradually stir in reserved cooking liquid. Bring mixture to a boil, stirring constantly. Reduce heat and simmer 1 minute.
- Remove from heat. Stir in fish, onion and sour cream. Mix well.
- Spoon mixture into pie shell. Bake 50 to 55 minutes or until crust is golden.
- Let stand at room temperature for 15 minutes before serving.
- Garnish with lemon slices and chopped parsley.

Preparation Note: This serves 4-6. You will need 2 pies for 8 people.

Tossed Salad with Paprika Dressing
(Serves 8)

1 head of lettuce
4 green onions, diced
4 tomatoes, chopped

½ lb. fresh mushrooms, sliced
1 recipe Paprika Dressing (below)

- Place lettuce, onions, tomatoes and mushrooms in salad bowl. When ready to serve, pour Dressing over salad or set salad on table and let the guests help themselves.

Paprika Dressing
(Yields approximately 1 cup)

¾ cup oil
¼ cup vinegar
½ tsp. salt

1 tsp. paprika
1 tsp. sugar (optional)
½ tsp. garlic powder or 1 clove of fresh garlic

- Combine all ingredients in a jar. Shake and chill.
- Remove clove of garlic before serving.

Honeydew Melon
(Serves 8)

4 medium honeydew melons
2 cups orange juice

1 cup honey

- Cut melons in half and remove seeds.
- Make melon balls and place in bowl.
- Combine orange juice and honey and pour over melon balls.
- Chill for 1 hour.

Poppy Swirl
(Oven 350°)

½ cup butter or margarine
¼ cup sugar
1 tsp. salt
2 envelopes active dry yeast
1 tsp. sugar

¾ cup very warm water
1 tsp. grated lemon rind
3 cups flour
1 recipe Poppy Seed Filling (below)

- Combine butter, sugar and salt in a small saucepan; heat slowly, stirring often, until butter melts. Cool to lukewarm.
- Dissolve yeast and 1 tsp. sugar in very warm water in a large bowl. (Very warm water should feel comfortably warm when dropped on wrist.) Stir until well blended and allow to stand 10 minutes or until mixture begins to bubble.
- Stir in cooled butter mixture and lemon rind.
- Beat in enough flour to make a soft dough; turn out onto a lightly floured surface. Knead until smooth and elastic, about 5 minutes, using enough flour to keep from sticking.
- Place in a buttered bowl. Cover with a clean towel or plastic wrap. Let rise in a warm place, away from draft, approximately 1 hour or until double in bulk.
- Punch dough down. Turn out onto lightly floured surface; knead a few times. Roll out to a 20″ x 16¼″ rectangle or two 10″ x 8″ rectangles. Spread with Poppy Seed Filling; roll up jelly-roll fashion, starting with long end.
- Place seam side down on a large greased cookie sheet, turn ends outward in the shape of a horseshoe.
- Make cuts 1″ apart, to within ½″ of centre of roll; twist pieces outward to show swirls. Cover dough; let rise in a warm place for 45 minutes or until almost double in bulk. Brush with a little beaten egg (if you wish).
- Bake in moderate oven 20 to 25 minutes, or until bread is a rich golden brown.
- Cool on cookie sheet 5 minutes, then loosen bread from sheet with a long spatula and slide onto a large rack to cool completely.

Serving Suggestion: Can be decorated with a glaze made with 1 cup sifted icing sugar combined with 1 tbsp. water.

Poppy Seed Filling
½ cup poppy seeds
¼ cup raisins
4 tbsp. milk
1 tbsp. soft butter

3 tbsp. honey
⅛ tsp. cinnamon
½ tsp. grated lemon rind

- Grind poppy seeds in coffee grinder or small blender container.
- Mix all ingredients in saucepan and bring to a boil. Simmer a couple of minutes and remove from heat. Cool before using in bread.

March Break is for Kids

8

Pack-A-Lunch
"50's" Birthday Party
Slumber Party
First Mixed Party
"Mommy I Don't Feel So Good"

Chapter Eight: March Break Is For Kids
Pack-A-Lunch
"50's" Birthday Party
Slumber Party
First Mixed Party
"Mommy I Don't Feel So Good"

March Break Is For Kids

With the coming of March Break, all moms will be busy planning and preparing various activities for the kids. The younger ones may be encouraged to take part in the programmes at the local Y.M.C.A., and the older ones could share in the preparations for a party at home. There's lots to do for kids of all ages during the March Break if you take the time to plan ahead with them.

Kids love parties, and they can learn what entertaining is all about when you let them plan their own party. Encourage them to give careful thought to what games might be played, what decorations should be made, and most important, what food should be served. In this chapter, we offer a few ideas.

For fun outside the home, we suggest that you inquire at your local Y.M.C.A. or library. In the town of Midland, a detailed programme for youngsters is offered at the Y, including outings to various cities and towns, sports events, and handicraft classes. The Y pool offers swimming and there is also skating at the arena. The Library usually plans a programme with films and displays for children. For the older children in Midland, the ski hills and cross country trails are just around the corner. They can pack a lunch for a day's outing, and we'll give them some ideas for what is tasty, nutritious, and easy to make.

At some time or another, the day will come when you will hear that familiar plea, "Mommy, I don't feel so good!"—It's always a good idea to have a few favourite recipes on hand when a little one is at home with a cold or just feeling under the weather. Kids love a little extra attention when they are feeling low; so cheer them up with a nice fluffy omelet or a soothing Peach Frosty. It's also a good idea to keep on hand a box full of special games, books, and crafts. Some children will be content to watch television or listen to records, but others may enjoy colouring or painting quietly to pass the time. Various puzzles may attract the attention of the older children, and for the wee ones, we have included a special recipe for that all time favourite, Play Dough.

We think kids are very special people. This chapter is designed with all our special friends in mind.

Chocolate Birthday Cake, page 165. "50's Birthday Party", page 162.

Pack-A-Lunch
Peanut Butter and Banana Rollups
Celery Boats
Granola Bars
Maple Walnut Creams
Hot Chocolate

Peanut Butter and Banana Rollups
(Yields 1 rollup)

butter   peanut butter
bread   banana

- Butter slice of bread and spread with peanut butter.
- Slice banana lengthwise and cut in half. Place banana slice on top of peanut butter and roll sandwich. Wrap in Saran or foil.

Celery Boats

celery stalks   peanut butter or cheese spread

- Spoon peanut butter or cheese spread into the celery boat and spread. Wrap in Saran.

Granola Bars
(Oven 350°)

1 cup margarine   1 tsp. baking soda
1½ cups brown sugar   1 cup oatmeal
2 eggs, slightly beaten   2 cups granola
1½ tsp. vanilla   ½ cup chopped nuts
1½ cups flour   1 cup raisins

- Cream margarine until smooth.
- Add sugar and eggs. Mix well.
- Add remaining ingredients and press into a 9" x 9" cake pan.
- Bake about 50 to 60 minutes. While still warm, cut into bars. (Can also be made into drop cookies—bake 12 to 15 minutes.)

Maple Walnut Creams
(Yields 2 lbs.)

1 cup white sugar
2 cups brown sugar
⅛ tsp. salt
2 tbsp. corn syrup

¾ cup milk
¼ cup butter
1½ tsp. vanilla
1 cup chopped walnuts

- Combine sugars, salt, corn syrup, milk and butter. Bring to a boil.
- Cook over medium heat to 238° (soft ball stage). Remove from heat and cool to luke-warm. Do not stir.
- Oil an 8″ x 8″ pan.
- Add vanilla and beat until mixture begins to thicken. Mix in walnuts and beat until candy loses its gloss.
- Quickly spread into a pan and let set. Cut.

Hot Chocolate
(1 serving)

¾ cup milk
2 tsp. chocolate syrup or instant chocolate

marshmallows

- Measure milk and chocolate into a saucepan. Heat until bubbles form.
- Top with marshmallows.

Serving Suggestion: If you are taking the hot chocolate in a thermos, take the marshmallows along in a plastic bag. Float marshmallows on top of drinks once they have been poured from thermos.

Another idea which the kids will like is to buy them their own wineskins to take their favourite drinks in for skiing and skating outings.

"50's" Birthday Party

(For 8)

French Fries
Hamburgers
Chocolate Birthday Cake
Cherry Coke

"50's Birthday Party

"50's, glorious 50's". Share part of that glorious era with your children. Here is a party we planned for a ninth birthday. It can be adapted for any occasion; for older children, teens and adults. Don't forget the bubble gum!

Because of the popularity of the movie "Grease", we called it a "Grease Party."

(a) *Invitations:*

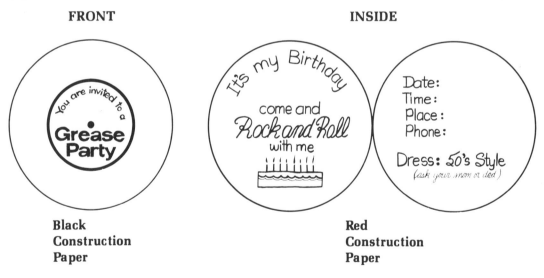

(b) *Decor:* For real authenticity, chicken wire and kleenex flowers are a must. Construct a rainbow, star, or large football with the chicken wire and stuff holes with kleenex flowers of the appropriate colours.

Music: There must be lots of good old fashioned Rock 'n' Roll music; so ask around; there will be people who have a good collection of appropriate music.

Dress: Felt skirts, pedal pushers, pleated skirts and bobby socks.

Activities: (1) Dancing—teach guests to jive. Throw in a bit of the Popeye and the old two-step waltz. Don't forget, girls sat along one wall and boys along the other. We always had a comb and went to the washroom in groups!

(2) Doughnut Eating Contest—Suspend doughnuts from a string. Pair off guests in twos. Place one on each side of doughnut. When pairs are lined up on each side of their doughnut, give the 'go' signal. Object is to see which team eats the entire doughnut first and not have it fall to the floor.

(3) Spin the Bottle—Ask participants to stand in a circle and place an empty bottle in centre. Spin the bottle. When the bottle stops, the person to whom the bottle is pointing has to suffer the consequences. When we played this we spun the bottle a second time to see who we kissed.

Other suggestions are: (a) Have a bag of different articles of clothing. When the bottle points to an individual, that person has to reach into the bag and put on whatever he or she pulls out. (b) When the bottle points at someone, that person has to sing a song or do a dance. The bottle is put into motion again by the person to whom the bottle has just pointed.

(4) Place the Disc on the Record—This is played similar to 'pin the tail on the donkey'. With a large sheet of black construction paper, cut out a large circle representing a record. With different coloured construction paper cut out several small circles representing the discs placed in 45s. Place masking tape or Scotch tape on the back of the coloured discs, looping the tape to have a sticky back. Hang the record on the wall. Blindfold each person. Spin them around a couple of times and point them in the direction of the record. They are to hold disc with sticky side out. The person moves towards the record and places the disc where they touch. The person who gets the disc closest to the centre of the record wins.

(5) Toss the platter—Decorate a couple of pieces of cardboard or small paper plates, each to look like a 45 record. Place a string across the platter as in discus throwing. Measure who throws the farthest.

(6) Penny Throw—Decorate a box to look like a turntable with a 45 on top. Cut out a hole the size of the centre of a 45. Give each person five pennies. Have them stand in an appointed place and throw pennies, attempting to get them in the hole. Give a small prize for each successful throw.

(7) Hat Decorating—Have on hand aluminum pie plates, paper plates or large party hats, ribbons, crêpe paper, egg cartons, streamers or any other things you can think of— don't forget a stapler and glue. Each person is to decorate an original hat. Allow a reasonable amount of time. (This also gives you a chance to get the meal on the way.) We took a Polaroid picture of each child with their hats and tucked these in their goodie bags. Prizes can be awarded for whatever categories you choose.

French Fries

When preparing French Fries for a group, the two stage frying method is the most efficient.

1 large potato per serving   vegetable oil for deep fryer
ice water

- Peel and slice potatoes into strips about ⅜" thick. Place in ice water for 10 to 15 minutes. Wipe well with a towel to remove excess moisture and starch.
- Preheat vegetable oil in deep fryer 300° to 330°.
- Place potatoes in hot oil, about one cup at a time and cook 2 minutes or until splattering has stopped. Remove and place on paper towelling. Let cool.
- Just before serving, heat oil to 375°. Finish frying potatoes for 3 minutes or until golden brown. Drain on paper towels.

Hamburgers
(Serves 8)

3 lb. hamburg   2 tbsp. water
2 eggs   3 tbsp. wheat germ
2 tbsp. ketchup   16 buns
1 tbsp. mustard

- Place first six ingredients in a large bowl. Mix thoroughly and shape into 16 patties.
- Place on a platter or cookie sheet with wax paper between layers and refrigerate until needed.
- Broil approximately 8 minutes on each side or until brown.
- Heat buns and serve.

Serving Suggestions: Depending on individual preferences: (a) place a slice of cheese on each meat patty the last minute of broiling; (b) make twice as many patties from the same amount of meat, making each very thin. Place grated cheese (Mozzarella or Swiss) in centre of each patty. Top with second patty and pinch edges together.

Condiments

vinegar   onions
ketchup   lettuce
mustard   pickles
relish   tomatoes

Chocolate Birthday Cake
(Yields two 8″ layers, Oven 325°)

½ cup shortening
1 cup sugar
2 eggs, well beaten
2 squares unsweetened chocolate,
  melted
½ tsp. vanilla

1½ cups flour
¾ tsp. baking soda
½ tsp. salt
1 cup sour milk

- Cream shortening and blend in sugar. Beat until fluffy.
- Add eggs; beat until well combined.
- Add melted chocolate and vanilla.
- Blend dry ingredients together and add to creamed mixture, alternating with the sour milk.
- Pour batter into greased pans. Bake 30 to 35 minutes.

Preparation Note: To make sour milk, add 1 tbsp. vinegar to 1 cup warm milk. Let mixture stand for 10 minutes.

Butter Frosting
6 tbsp. butter, softened
1 tsp. vanilla

4 cups icing sugar
4-5 tbsp. warm milk

- Cream butter and beat in vanilla.
- Blend in icing sugar alternately with warm milk. Beat until smooth and of spreading consistency. Add more milk or more icing sugar, if necessary.

Decorating the cake: Ice cake with butter frosting. Use construction paper or coloured frosting for disc in the centre. Write an appropriate greeting on disc and place a sparkler in centre as post on turntable.

Cherry Coke
(Serves 1)

1 tsp. cherry or maraschino syrup   Coke

- In an 8 oz. glass, place a teaspoon of syrup flavouring and fill with coke.
- Add ice, stir and serve.

Preparation Note: For adults only: Amaretto, cherry wine or brandy are excellent substitutes in cherry coke.

Slumber Party
(For 8)
Grape Juice Fizz
Finger Salad and Dip
Mini Pizzas
Crunchy Cake

Grape Juice Fizz
(Serves 8)

1 quart ginger ale   1 pint of grape juice

- Mix the ginger ale and grape juice in a large container.
- Serve with ice.

Finger Salad and Dip
(Serves 8)

Raw vegetables of your choice to serve 8:

cucumber slices   fresh mushrooms
green pepper slices   celery sticks
tomatoes   cauliflower flowerets
radishes   carrot sticks
green onions

- Clean all vegetables and prepare in slices or sticks.
- Arrange on a large serving tray with the dip in the centre.

Preparation Note: If you prepare vegetables the day before, keep in plastic bags.

Dip
4 oz. cream cheese, softened   ¼ tsp. dill weed
½ cup sour cream   pepper
½ cup mayonnaise   pinch of rosemary
⅛ cup finely chopped green onion   Worcestershire sauce to taste

- Combine cream cheese, sour cream and mayonnaise and beat well.
- Add remaining ingredients and blend.

Mini Pizzas
(Serves 8)

12 English muffins
8 oz. tomato sauce
1 onion, finely chopped
1 medium pepperoni, thinly sliced
salt and pepper to taste
oregano

1 10oz. can mushroom pieces, drained
1 green pepper, chopped
¼ lb. Mozzarella cheese, grated

- Slice English muffins in half and toast.
- Spread each muffin half with tomato sauce.
- Top with onion, pepperoni, salt, pepper, oregano, mushrooms, green pepper and Mozzarella cheese.
- Place under broiler until the cheese melts.

Preparation Note: Set all ingredients out on the counter and let the guests assemble their own pizzas.

Crunchy Cake
(Serves 8-10)

1 Angel food cake, chilled
4-5 "Crispy Crunch" chocolate bars, chilled
1 pint whipping cream

1 tsp. sugar
1 tsp. vanilla

- Place cake on a flat surface. With a sharp knife or piece of thread, slice cake in three equal layers. Refrigerate.
- Chop chocolate bars in food processor a few seconds. (Do not process too long; bars should be broken down into small chunks, not crumbs.)
- In a large mixing bowl, beat whipping cream until it begins to thicken. Add sugar and vanilla. Continue beating until whipping cream holds its shape in peaks.
- Gently fold chopped chocolate bars into whipping cream.
- Spread mixture generously between layers, and over top and sides of angel food cake. Chill and serve.

First Mixed Party
(For 8)
Banana Shake
Rye Sandwich
Chocolate Fondue

Banana Shake
(Serves 2)

1½ cups milk
1 banana, mashed

1 tbsp. sugar or honey
¼ tsp. vanilla

- Process milk, banana, sugar and vanilla in blender until smooth. Serve at once.

Rye Sandwich
(1 Sandwich)

1 slice rye bread
butter
1 slice ham

1 slice cheese
1 slice pineapple
cherry

- Toast rye bread slightly.
- Butter toast and top with ham, cheese and pineapple ring. Top with a cherry.
- Toast under broiler until cheese melts.

Chocolate Fondue
(Serves 6-8)

¼ cup whipping cream
1 bar (3 oz.) milk chocolate
fruit pieces of your choice—apples,
  oranges, pineapple, bananas, grapes,
  cherries

marshmallows, cake, and nuts can
  also be dipped.

- Warm the cream carefully in a small saucepan or chafing dish.
- Break the chocolate into the cream and stir until melted and smooth. Place chafing dish on table.
- Arrange your fruit on a platter and use fondue forks to dip the fruit into the chocolate.

Serving Suggestion: chocolate begins to thicken as it cools. Place your dish in hot water to keep from thickening too quickly.

_____ "Mommy, I Don't Feel So Good" _____

Fruit Juice Popsicles
Graham Shake
Peach Frosty
Cheese Soufflé
Fluffy Omelet
Macaroni and Cheese
Ice Cream and Hot Chocolate Sauce
Dream Cocktail
Bran Muffins
Aunt Rena's Great Custard
Rice Pudding For One
Play Dough

Fruit Juice Popsicles

fruit juices, frozen or canned: apple, orange, grape

- Pour fruit juices into popsicle tray and freeze.

Graham Shake
(Yields 3 cups)

4 graham wafers, broken
1½ cups cold milk

1 tbsp. honey
1 pint chocolate ice cream

- Combine ingredients and blend until smooth. Serve with a straw.

Peach Frosty
(Yields 3¾ cups)

1 cup cold milk
1 14oz. can peaches, drained

1 tsp. lemon juice
1 pint vanilla ice cream

- Combine ingredients and blend until smooth.

Cheese Soufflé
(Serves 3, Oven 350°)

2 tbsp. butter
2 tbsp. flour
¼ tsp. salt
pepper
¼ tsp. dry mustard

⅔ cup milk
⅔ cup shredded cheddar cheese
2 egg yolks, well beaten
2 egg whites
¼ tsp. cream of tartar

- Melt butter in heavy saucepan and blend in flour, seasonings and milk. Cook over medium heat, stirring constantly until mixture comes to a boil.
- Add cheese, stirring until cheese melts.
- Stir in egg yolks.
- Beat egg whites and cream of tartar until stiff. Fold in the cheese mixture.
- Pour into ungreased 1 quart baking dish and bake about 50 minutes until golden brown.

Fluffy Omelet
(Serves 4, Oven 350°)

4 eggs, separated
4 tbsp. hot water

salt and pepper
1 tbsp. oil

- Beat egg whites until stiff.
- Beat yolks until thick. Add hot water, pepper and salt.
- Fold mixtures together.
- Heat oil in oven proof skillet. Cook egg mixture over low heat until omelet is puffy. Place in oven until top of omelet is dry (about 10 minutes). Serve immediately.

Macaroni and Cheese
(Serves 4-6, Oven 350°)

1 cup macaroni
¼ cup butter
1 tbsp. chopped onion
¼ cup flour
salt and pepper to taste

¼ tsp. dry mustard
2 cups milk
1 cup cheddar cheese, shredded
⅔ cup bread or cracker crumbs

- Cook macaroni in boiling salted water according to package directions. Drain.
- Melt butter and sauté onion.
- Blend in flour, salt, pepper and mustard.
- Gradually stir in milk stirring constantly until thickened.
- Add cheese and stir.
- Mix cheese mixture and macaroni together in a two quart casserole. Top with crumbs. Bake 30 minutes.

Ice Cream and Hot Chocolate Sauce
(Serves 6-8)

1 pkg. chocolate pudding powder   1 pint vanilla ice cream

- Prepare chocolate pudding and cook according to directions on the package.
- Spoon ice cream into bowls and top with hot chocolate pudding. Eat right away!

Dream Cocktail
(Serves 8)

1 cup cooked rice   1 cup coloured marshmallows
1 cup fruit cocktail, drained   squirt of lemon juice
1 cup crushed pineapple, drained   1 cup whipping cream
½ cup chopped nuts (optional)

- Mix together the rice, fruits, nuts, marshmallows and lemon juice. Chill.
- Whip cream and fold into rice and fruit. Chill until ready to serve.

Bran Muffins
(Yields 1 dozen muffins, Oven 400°)

¼ cup butter, softened   1 cup flour
¾ cup brown sugar   ⅓ tsp. salt
1 egg, beaten   1 tsp. soda
1 cup milk   1 tsp. baking powder
1 cup bran   ¼ cup raisins, coated with flour

- Cream butter and brown sugar.
- Add egg, milk and bran.
- In a separate bowl combine flour, salt, soda and baking powder.
- Add dry mixture to egg and butter mixture.
- Stir in flour coated raisins.
- Spoon into greased muffin tins and bake 15 to 20 minutes.

Aunt Rena's Great Custard
(Serves 6, Oven 350°)

3 large eggs   dash of salt
2 tbsp. sugar   ½ tsp. vanilla
2 cups milk   nutmeg

- Beat eggs and add sugar, milk, salt and vanilla; blend.
- Pour into buttered casserole dish and sprinkle with nutmeg.
- Place casserole in pan of water about 1" deep and bake in oven for 1 hour.

Rice Pudding For One
(Serves 1, Oven 350°)

¾ cup water
pinch of salt
¼ cup long grain rice
¼ cup milk
4 tsp. sugar

¼ tsp. vanilla
1 egg
2 tbsp. raisins
1 tsp. butter

- Bring water and salt to a boil and add rice. Cover and reduce heat to low. Cook until water has been absorbed (about 20 minutes).
- Rinse rice with cold water and drain.
- In a small bowl mix milk, sugar, vanilla, egg and raisins.
- Add rice to liquid mixture and mix well.
- Pour into a small buttered baking dish. Bake uncovered for approximately 20 minutes. Serve hot or cold.

Serving Suggestion: Nice with cream or milk.

Play Dough

1 cup of salt
1½ cups flour
¾ cup water

5 tbsp. oil
food colouring

- Mix together and store in the refrigerator.

Easter

Shrove Tuesday
Good Friday
Resurrection Brunch
Easter Get Together
Family Easter
Dinner for 12 Good Friends

Chapter Nine: Easter

Shrove Tuesday
Good Friday
Resurrection Brunch
Easter Get Together
Family Easter
Dinner for 12 Good Friends

Easter

Easter is a time of rebirth: the snow begins to melt, the sun is often warm and bright, and in sheltered areas, crocuses are popping through the ground. Soon the Georgian Bay woodlands will be gently covered in a blanket of trilliums—a sure sign that spring is on its way.

The Easter season starts with Shrove Tuesday, 40 days before Holy Week. Shrove Tuesday is often referred to as Pancake Tuesday, and it is on this occasion that many churches hold their annual pancake supper. St. Mark's Anglican Church in Midland hosts just such a pancake feast where the whole family can share in good food and good fellowship. If you prefer to have friends drop in to your home for Pancake Tuesday, we have included some of our favourite pancake recipes.

When Good Friday arrives, the family often gets together in the kitchen to bake Hot Cross Buns and decorate Easter Eggs. Both can be enjoyable activities for all, and just to help out, we offer you our own recipes and ideas in this Easter chapter. When the eggs are decorated, brightly coloured baskets can be made from construction paper to use in the Easter Egg Hunt on Easter Sunday morning. Filled baskets may then make pretty centre-pieces for the breakfast table, or for the family dinner table.

Easter Sunday dinner is always an enjoyable family get-together. Over a delicious meal, family members may discuss the past winter's events, and share thoughts about the coming of spring.

Happiness is a family together at Easter. Happy Easter.

Shrove Tuesday

Orange Wholewheat Pancakes
(Serves 4-6)

2 eggs
¼ cup oil
2 cups whole wheat flour

½ tsp. soda
1½-2 cups orange juice

- Beat eggs and oil together.
- Sift together flour and soda; add to the eggs.
- Gradually add orange juice to obtain desired consistency.
- Fry in a medium hot, greased pan.

Preparation Note: Pancakes should not be beaten, merely moisten dry ingredients. They are best mixed a few hours ahead and left to rest. For best results, pour batter from tip of a spoon into hot, greased pan. Allow to cook 2 to 3 minutes, until bubbles appear on surface before turning to cook other side. They should be a nice golden brown.

Yoghurt Wholewheat Pancakes
(Serves 4-6)

2 eggs
1½ tbsp. honey
1½ cups yoghurt

1½ cups whole wheat flour
3 tsp. baking powder
1 Topping recipe (below)

- Beat eggs.
- Add honey and yoghurt; mix well.
- Add dry ingredients and mix.
- Fry in hot greased pan.

Topping
1 cup cream cheese
1 tbsp. lemon juice

1 tbsp. honey

- Combine Topping ingredients and spread over pancakes.

Sour Cream Pancakes
(Serves 4)

1 cup flour
½ tsp. salt
½ tsp. soda

1⅓ cups sour cream
1 egg, slightly beaten

- Sift dry ingredients.
- Combine sour cream and egg and add to dry ingredients. Stir to moisten; do not beat.
- Fry in hot, greased pan.

Good Friday

Hot Cross Buns
(Yields 18 buns, Oven 375°)

Traditionally, Hot Cross Buns baked on Good Friday are believed to have special curative powers.

1 pkg. active dry yeast
4-5 cups flour
⅓ cup sugar
½ tsp. salt
1¼ tsp. cinnamon
½ tsp. nutmeg
¼ tsp. cloves
1 cup milk

¼ cup butter
2 eggs, room temperature
1 cup currants or raisins
4 oz. candied citron, chopped
1 egg yolk
3 tbsp. water
1 recipe Frosting (below)

- Prepare yeast as per package directions.
- In a large bowl, thoroughly mix 1½ cups flour, sugar, salt and spices.
- Heat milk and butter in saucepan over low heat until warm (110°F).
- Gradually add milk to dry ingredients.
- Add yeast and beat 2 minutes with electric mixer at medium speed, scraping bowl occasionally.
- Add eggs and ½ cup flour (or enough to make a thick batter) and beat at high speed for 2 minutes scraping bowl occasionally.
- Gradually stir in 2 cups flour to make a soft dough, adding any additional flour 2 tablespoons at a time, if needed. (Dough should be soft, not stiff).
- Turn dough out onto lightly floured surface and knead until smooth and elastic, about 8 to 10 minutes (5 minutes with a dough hook).
- Place in oiled bowl, turning to coat top of dough. Cover with plastic wrap and a towel wrung out in hot water. Allow to rise in warm place until doubled in bulk (about 1 hour).
- Punch dough down and turn out onto lightly floured surface. Knead in currants and citron.
- Divide into 18 equal pieces, forming each piece into a ball, and place in two well oiled 9″ round cake pans.
- Combine 1 egg yolk and 2 tablespoons of water to make an egg wash. Brush buns with egg wash. Cover with waxed paper and allow to rise in a warm place until doubled in size (about 1¼ hours).
- Put a cross on top of each bun with a razor blade or scissors. Bake 20 to 25 minutes or until golden.
- Remove from pans and cool on wire racks.
- Combine Frosting ingredients and form cross on top of buns.

Frosting
1 cup icing sugar
1 tsp. lemon juice

1 tbsp. hot milk
½ tsp. vanilla

Easter Eggs
(Yields 12-18 eggs)

1 recipe Fondant Centre (below)   1 recipe Ornamental Icing (below)
1 recipe Dipping Chocolate (below)

Fondant Centre

½ lb. white margarine   1 can Eagle Brand condensed milk
1 tbsp. vanilla   3 lbs. icing sugar
1 tbsp. salt   yellow food colouring

- Cream together margarine, vanilla and salt.
- Add condensed milk and beat until smooth.
- Gradually add icing sugar. When mixture becomes too stiff to stir, mix in remaining icing sugar by kneading with your hands. Continue kneading for approximately 15 minutes, until paste is very smooth.
- Divide fondant equally into three parts.
- Colour one portion with yellow food colouring for yolk. Leave other two white.
- Divide yellow fondant into 12 to 18 equal portions. Divide each white portion into same amounts. Shape yellow fondant portions into egg yolks and surround each yolk with 2 white portions. Mould to form the shape of an egg.
- Set moulded eggs onto wax paper lined pans and refrigerate several hours before dipping. Best if allowed to set for a day.

Dipping Chocolate

1 lb. semi-sweet chocolate   3 oz. paraffin wax

- Place chocolate and wax in top of double boiler and allow to melt, stirring occasionally.
- Dip eggs one at a time completely covering one side at a time. Chocolate should be returned to heat frequently to keep chocolate shiny.
- Decorate with Ornamental Frosting once chocolate has hardened.

Ornamental Frosting

3 egg whites   ¼ tsp. cream of tartar
1 lb. + 1 cup sifted icing sugar

- Place egg whites in a large mixing bowl and add 2 tbsp. icing sugar. Beat 3 minutes with electric mixer at medium speed.
- Repeat until 1½ cups of icing sugar is used.
- Add cream of tartar.
- Continue adding icing sugar by spoonsful until frosting is stiff enough to hold its shape. Cut with knife; if frosting remains parted, it is the right consistency.
- Force frosting through pastry tube to make desired shapes.

Resurrection Brunch
(For 6)
Rise and Shine Cocktail
Melon Balls with Lime
French Toast
Grilled Canadian Bacon
(Coffee)

Rise and Shine Cocktail
(Serves 6)

6 jiggers tequilla or coffee liqueur   12 orange wedges
24 oz. orange juice

- In a large glass, place a jigger of liqueur and 6 oz. of orange juice. Garnish with orange wedges.

Melon Balls with Lime
(Serves 6)

1 large ripe honeydew melon   12 oz. 7-Up or soda
1 ripe cantaloup   6 wedges fresh lime
1 cup dry white wine

- Slice melon and cantaloup in half and discard seeds.
- Using a melon baller, carefully scoop out the fruit of the melon and cantaloup.
- Place fruits in a bowl and toss with wine. Refrigerate an hour or so.
- To serve, divide into individual fruit bowls and cover fruits with 7-Up or soda water. Serve with a wedge of lime.

French Toast
(Serves 6, Oven 400°)

3 thick slices egg bread   1 cup whipping cream
oil   ¼ tsp. salt
4 eggs   ¼ cup icing sugar

- Slice egg bread approximately ¾″ thick. Remove crusts and slice diagonally into wedges.
- Place ½″ oil in skillet and heat to 325°.
- Beat together eggs, cream and salt.
- Dip each slice of bread in egg mixture, allowing it to soak up as much liquid as possible.
- Fry bread in hot oil until brown, turning only once.
- Transfer to baking sheet and place in oven and bake until puffed up, 3 to 5 minutes.
- Drain on paper towelling. Sprinkle lightly with icing sugar and serve.

Serving Suggestion: Serve with side dishes of applesauce, sour cream or maple syrup.

Grilled Canadian Bacon
(Serves 6)

1 lb. Canadian bacon   1 tbsp. butter

• Slice bacon and fry in butter approximately 3 minutes on each side.

Preparation Note: Canadian bacon is often referred to as Peameal bacon.

MENU

Easter Get Together
(For 6)
Polynesian Pineapple Chicken
Pineapple Rice
Creamy String Beans
Rice and Peas
Orange Baked Alaskas

Polynesian Pineapple Chicken
(Serves 6, Oven 350°)

3-3½ lbs. chicken pieces   ½ cup sliced green pepper
salt, pepper, paprika to taste   3 tbsp. soy sauce
10 oz. can consommé, undiluted   ¼ lb. mushrooms
19 oz. can pineapple chunks

• Pat chicken pieces dry and place in lightly buttered pan.
• Sprinkle with salt, pepper and paprika.
• Add consommé and bake covered for 45 minutes.
• Add drained pineapple chunks, green peppers and soy sauce and bake an additional
  20 minutes, or until tender.
• Sauté mushrooms and add during the last few minutes of cooking.

Pineapple Rice
(Serves 6)

1½ cups pineapple juice   1½ cups instant rice

• Bring pineapple juice to a boil.
• Stir in rice, remove from heat and let stand for 5 to 10 minutes.
• Fluff with a fork.

Serving Suggestion: This is to be served as a side dish with the Rice and Peas.

Rice and Peas

(Serves 6)

4 cloves
4 whole black peppers
4 cardamon seeds (husks removed)
½ tsp. cumin seeds
2 bay leaves
1 cinnamon stick

2 cups water
1 cup long grain rice
½ of a 10oz. pkg. frozen peas
2 tbsp. butter
salt and pepper to taste

- Make a spice bag out of cheese cloth and tie cloves, peppers, cardamon, cumin, bay leaves and cinnamon into it.
- Place spice bag in 2 cups of water and bring to a boil. Turn heat off and squeeze out bag.
- Bring spiced water to a boil again and add long grain rice. Cook approximately 25 minutes or until done.
- Steam peas.
- When rice is cooked, add cooked peas, butter, pepper and salt. Fluff with a fork.

Creamy String Beans

(Serves 6, Oven 350°)

½ cup diced celery
½ cup diced onion
2 tbsp. butter
1 10oz. pkg. frozen string beans
 (or broccoli)

3 oz. grated cheese
1 can cream of mushroom soup
½ cup cooked rice

- Sauté celery and onion in butter.
- Steam frozen beans (or broccoli).
- Mix cheese with 1 can mushroom soup. Heat until smooth and creamy.
- Place all ingredients in a casserole and bake in oven for 30 minutes.

Orange Baked Alaskas

(Serves 6)

6 large oranges
1 pint orange sherbet
3 egg whites

⅓ cup sugar
¼ tsp. cream of tartar

- Slice tops from oranges and scoop out the orange shells.
- Fill with orange sherbet and freeze until firm (at least 5 hours).
- Beat egg whites with sugar and cream of tartar until stiff.
- Top each orange with meringue and brown under the broiler for a few minutes.

Preparation Note: These can be prepared earlier in the day and placed in the freezer until you are ready to serve them.

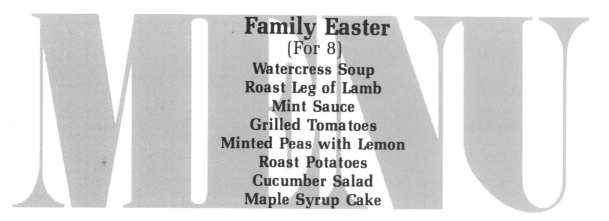

Family Easter
(For 8)
Watercress Soup
Roast Leg of Lamb
Mint Sauce
Grilled Tomatoes
Minted Peas with Lemon
Roast Potatoes
Cucumber Salad
Maple Syrup Cake

Watercress Soup
(Serves 8)

2 bunches watercress
2 onions, diced
4 tbsp. butter
1 large potato, diced

6 cups chicken broth
salt and pepper
2 cups light cream

- Chop watercress, reserving 8 sprigs.
- In soup kettle sauté onion in butter.
- Add potatoes, watercress and chicken broth; season to taste with salt and pepper.
- Cook covered until potatoes are done.
- Purée soup in batches in blender or food processor.
- Return to pot, reheat; add light cream and mix well.
- To serve, garnish each bowl with a sprig of watercress.

Roast Leg of Lamb
(Serves 8, Oven 450°)

5 lb. leg of lamb, room temperature
2 garlic cloves, crushed
½ lemon

1 tsp. rosemary
1 tsp. thyme

- Remove lamb from refrigerator 1 hour before cooking.
- Rub meat with garlic, lemon and rosemary.
- Insert garlic pieces under the skin using a sharp knife.
- Sprinkle lamb well with rosemary and thyme.
- Place meat fat side up on a rack in an uncovered pan and place in 450° oven.
- Immediately reduce heat to 350° and cook 25 minutes per pound or until internal thermometer reaches 175 to 180°. Lamb is nicer rare than well done.
- Occasionally baste with lemon juice.
- Pour off fat and use the lemon drippings to serve as a sauce.
- Carve roast parallel to the bone and serve hot.

Mint Sauce

1 cup mint leaves (dried or fresh)   ¼ cup icing sugar
1 cup vinegar

- Shake all ingredients in a jar.
- Cover and refrigerate for 24 hours before serving.

Grilled Tomatoes
(Serves 8, Oven 350°)

2 tbsp. butter   1 tsp. oregano
1 clove garlic, minced   thyme
1 cup bread crumbs   4 large tomatoes cut in half

- Melt butter in pan. Add garlic, bread crumbs and oregano.
- Sprinkle tomatoes with crushed thyme and place a layer of the crumb mixture on each tomato.
- Place tomatoes in oven for 25 minutes.
- Serve hot.

Minted Peas with Lemon
(Serves 8)

2 10oz. pkgs. frozen peas   1 tbsp. dried mint
3 tbsp. butter   2 tbsp. lemon juice

- Cook peas according to directions on package and drain.
- Add butter, mint and lemon and toss to coat.
- Heat through and serve.

Roast Potatoes
(Serves 8, Oven 350°)

8 large potatoes, peeled   paprika
cooking oil

- Cut potatoes in four.
- Coat with cooking oil and place in shallow baking dish.
- Sprinkle with paprika.
- Bake in oven until potatoes are done, approximately 1 hour.

Cucumber Salad
(Serves 8)

4 medium cucumbers
1 tsp. salt
6 green onions, chopped
1 tbsp. dill weed
4 tbsp. vinegar

1 tsp. salt
1 tsp. sugar
1 tsp. pepper
½ cup sour cream

- Groove cucumbers with fork and thinly slice. Place in a dish, sprinkle with salt and let stand 15 minutes.
- Drain. Press out water that has accumulated and place cucumbers in a serving bowl.
- Add the onions, dill, vinegar, salt, sugar and pepper.
- Toss well and refrigerate for 1 hour.
- Spread sour cream on top just before serving. Sprinkle with more dill and toss.

Maple Syrup Cake
(Oven 375°)

½ cup butter
½ cup sugar
¾ cup maple syrup
2 eggs, beaten
1 tsp. vanilla
2 cups flour

½ tsp. salt
2½ tsp. baking powder
½ cup pecans, chopped
1 recipe Soft Maple Icing (below)

- Blend butter, sugar, syrup, eggs and vanilla.
- Sift flour with salt and baking powder.
- Gradually add dry ingredients to butter and egg mixture, beating well after each addition.
- Stir in nuts.
- Pour into well greased pans and bake for 20 minutes.
- Carefully turn cakes onto racks to cool. Ice with Soft Maple Icing.

Soft Maple Icing

¼ cup soft butter
½ cup maple syrup

½ tsp. vanilla
2½ cups icing sugar

- Blend butter, syrup and vanilla until smooth.
- Gradually blend in icing sugar.

Dinner for 12 Good Friends
(For 12)
Glazed Ham
Potatoes Romanoff
Sautéed Beets
Devilled Parsnips
Waldorf Salad
Corn Bread
Citrus Chiffon Pie
Pineapple Bavarian Cream Pie

Glazed Ham
(Serves 12, Oven 325°)

1 10lb. cooked ham
¼ cup whole cloves
1 16oz. can pineapple slices
maraschino cherries

1 cup ginger ale
1 cup brown sugar
1 tbsp. dried mustard

- Score outside of ham in criss-cross cuts ¼″ deep, 1″ apart.
- Stud with cloves.
- Cover ham with pineapple slices with a cherry in the centre of each slice. (Secure pineapple slices and cherries with toothpicks.)
- Make glaze by mixing ginger ale, brown sugar and mustard together and baste ham.
- Bake ham 1½ hours.
- Baste with glaze often throughout cooking time.

Potatoes Romanoff
(Serves 12, Oven 350°)

6 cups cooked sliced potatoes
1½ cups cottage cheese
1½ cups sour cream
1½ cups cheddar cheese, diced

2½ cups milk
1 tsp. garlic salt
parsley to garnish

- Mix all ingredients thoroughly.
- Pour into buttered casserole and bake 1 hour.
- Sprinkle with parsley before serving.

Sautéed Beets
(Serves 12)

6 tbsp. butter
12 cooked beets, diced

salt and pepper to taste
parsley

- Melt butter in heavy saucepan and add beets, salt and pepper.
- Sauté, stirring constantly for 2 minutes.
- Sprinkle with parsley and serve.

Devilled Parsnips
(Serves 12)

12 medium parsnips, peeled and sliced
  lengthwise
½ cup butter, melted
3 tbsp. brown sugar
3 tbsp. wine vinegar
1 tsp. dry mustard

1 tsp. minced chives
¼ tsp. basil
salt and pepper
paprika

- Brown parsnips on both sides in melted butter over moderate heat, turning occasionally.
- Stir in brown sugar and vinegar, dry mustard, minced chives and basil. Salt and pepper to taste.
- Cover pan and simmer over moderate heat for about 20 minutes or until tender.
- Sprinkle with paprika when about to serve.

Waldorf Salad
(Serves 12)

5 cups diced tart apples
3 cups diced celery
1½ cups mayonnaise

2 tsp. Dijon mustard
salad greens
chopped walnuts

- Mix apples. celery, mayonnaise and mustard.
- Serve on greens.
- Garnish with chopped walnuts.

Cornbread
(Yields 9" loaf, Oven 400°)

1½ cups yellow cornmeal
1 cup flour
⅓ cup sugar
1 tsp. salt
1 tbsp. baking powder

2 eggs
6 tbsp. melted and cooled butter
6 tbsp. melted and cooled shortening
1½ cups milk

- In mixing bowl combine cornmeal, flour, sugar, salt and baking powder.
- In a separate bowl beat eggs lightly, add melted butter and shortening and stir in milk.
- Pour liquid mixture into bowl of dry ingredients and beat together for about a minute, or until smooth. Do not overbeat.
- Butter 9" loaf pan and pour in batter.
- Bake 45 minutes or until bread comes slightly away from edge of pan and is golden.

Citrus Chiffon Pie
(Yields 9" pie, Serves 6-8)

1 9" baked pastry shell (see Basics, page 212)
1 envelope (1 tbsp.) unflavoured gelatin
½ cup sugar
dash salt
4 egg yolks
½ cup lemon juice
½ cup orange juice
¼ cup water
½ tsp. grated lemon peel
½ tsp. grated orange peel
4 egg whites
⅓ cup sugar
½ cup whipping cream, whipped
1 orange, thinly sliced

- Thoroughly mix gelatin, ½ cup sugar and salt in saucepan.
- Beat egg yolks, fruit juices and water.
- Stir into gelatin mixture.
- Cook and stir over medium heat until mixture comes to a boil.
- Remove from heat and stir in peel.
- Chill, stirring occasionally, until mixture mounds slightly when dropped from a spoon.
- Beat egg whites until soft peaks form.
- Gradually add ⅓ cup sugar, beating to stiff peaks.
- Fold in gelatin mixture and spoon into cooled baked pastry shell.
- Trim with whipped cream and orange slices.

Pineapple Bavarian Cream Pie
(Yields 9" pie, Serves 6-8)

1 9" baked pastry shell (see Basics, page 212)
1 14oz. can crushed pineapple in juice
2 envelopes unflavoured gelatin
4 eggs, separated
½ cup sugar
¼ tsp. salt
1 cup milk
⅓ cup Kirsch
1 tsp. vanilla
⅔ cup sugar
1½ cup whipping cream
1 tbsp. icing sugar
¼ tsp. vanilla

- Drain pineapple. Measure ½ cup juice, pour juice into small bowl. Sprinkle gelatin over juice to soften. Let stand 5 minutes.
- Beat yolks in top part of double boiler. Stir in ½ cup sugar, salt, milk and softened gelatin. Cook over simmering water, stirring constantly, until mixture thickens and coats spoon. Remove from heat.
- Stir in Kirsch, vanilla and 1 cup drained pineapple. Pour mixture into a bowl. Place bowl in a larger bowl of ice water to speed setting. Chill, stirring often, until mixture thickens and mounds.
- Beat egg whites in a medium sized bowl until foamy white; slowly beat in remaining sugar until meringue forms stiff peaks.
- Beat 1 cup of whipping cream in small bowl until stiff.
- Fold meringue, then heavy cream into pineapple mixture until no streaks of white remain. Spoon into cooled pastry shell. Chill at least 2 hours or until set.
- Beat remaining ½ cup whipping cream with icing sugar and ¼ tsp. vanilla in a small bowl. Spoon remaining reserved pineapple in centre of pie; pipe whipped cream around pineapple and serve.

Spring Fare

A Touch of Maple
For the Sweet Tooth
After the Festival
Huronia Spring Pork
Ladies Spring Luncheon

Chapter Ten: Spring Fare
A Touch of Maple
For the Sweet Tooth
After the Festival
Huronia Spring Pork
Ladies Spring Luncheon

Spring Fare

Spring is in the air; so why not plan a pleasant spring outing with the family? We suggest a trip to the town of Elmvale (just 16 miles north of Barrie on Highway 27) for its Annual Maple Syrup Festival.

Now well known throughout the province of Ontario, the Elmvale Maple Syrup Festival first began in 1965 when a group of 16 townspeople gathered together to plan this spring event. Since then, the festival has captured the attention of many Elmvale citizens who take part in presenting a week of fun-filled activities and interesting attractions, free of charge to the public, in mid-April.

The heart and soul of the festival is truly evident when you meet at the sugar shacks outside of town and climb aboard a horse drawn wagon to ride through the beautiful hardwood bush. You can easily imagine the old days when sap was gathered in birch bark buckets, even though today's technology employs plastic tubing and vacuum pumps. Some maple syrup producers use metal buckets and others use a network of plastic pipes to gather sap directly from the trees into a storage tank. No matter how the sap is collected, it eventually ends up in the form of delicious pure maple syrup and it can be bought from the producers right at the bush.

During the festival, you can count on scheduled bus tours to the sugar bush, and when that wonderful fresh air gets your appetite going you can return to the Elmvale Community Centre for hot pancakes served with pure maple syrup. On the main street of town a pedestrian mall is set out so you can amble along at your leisure, stopping off at booths displaying hand crafts, furniture, art, home baking and canning, and of course, maple products. You'll see local entertainment along the way, with highlights such as square dancing, log sawing contests, and the selection of a Festival Queen. For the children, there are midway rides and a special area where farm and zoo animals are free to roam about.

We often think of maple syrup as that wonderful topping for pancakes or waffles. But the list of other uses for maple syrup is endless. You can top a fruit salad with it, or dress up a plain cake. The flavour of maple syrup can really add to a ham or to pork chops, and maple syrup drizzled over carrots or whirled into mashed potatoes makes a delightful change. Maple syrup is a versatile ingredient which we have incorporated into several recipes in this Springtime section.

There are many ways to celebrate the coming of Spring. We think there is nothing more enjoyable than a fine dinner with friends, or perhaps a luncheon get-together for the girls. With these ideas in mind, we have designed several Spring menus which are sure to please.

A Touch of Maple

(For 4)

Port Applesauce Mould
Cornish Hens and Rice with Orange Sauce
Baked Cauliflower
Maple Glazed Carrots
Maple Butter Tarts
Coffee

Port Applesauce Mould

(Serves 4)

1 pkg. raspberry jello
½ cup water
½ cup port wine, heated
1 tsp. lemon juice

1 tbsp. grated orange peel
16 oz. can applesauce, heated
½ cup sour cream

- Soften jello in water. Add hot port wine and stir until gelatin is dissolved.
- Add lemon juice, orange peel and hot applesauce.
- Let set until partially firm; add sour cream and mix well.
- Pour into an oiled mould. Chill until firm.
- Turn out on a plate.

Cornish Hens and Rice with Orange Sauce

(Serves 4, Oven 350°)

Hens
4 Cornish hens
salt
seedless green grapes

2 tbsp. butter, melted
1 recipe Rice (below)
1 recipe Orange Sauce (see next page)

- Wash hens and pat dry. Rub cavities with salt.
- Fill cavity with green seedless grapes.
- Place on a rack, breast side up, and brush with butter.
- Roast 40 minutes, brushing with butter occasionally.
- Increase temperature to 400° and cook 10 minutes longer.

Rice
3 cups Chicken Broth (see Basics,
    page 207)
½ tsp. salt
pinch of thyme

1 cup long grain rice
¾ cup sliced mushrooms

- Measure broth into saucepan; add salt and thyme. Bring to a boil.
- Add uncooked rice and mushrooms; bring to a boil. Reduce heat and simmer about 45 minutes or until the rice is cooked.

Sauce

⅔ cup raisins   1 tsp. salt
⅔ cup orange juice   ¼ tsp. paprika
¼ cup butter   ⅛ tsp. pepper
¼ cup flour   2 cups milk

- Combine raisins and orange juice in pan; heat to boiling point. Reduce heat and simmer 5 minutes. Set aside.
- In another saucepan melt butter; blend in flour, salt, paprika and pepper.
- Cook over low heat, stirring until the mixture is smooth.
- Remove from the heat and slowly stir in milk.
- Heat to boiling point and boil 1 minute.
- Gradually stir in raisins and orange juice mix.

Serving Suggestion: Place the hens on a bed of rice and pour some of the sauce over the hens. Serve the remaining sauce separately.

Baked Cauliflower
(Serves 4-6, Oven 375°)

1 head of cauliflower   2 tbsp. pimiento (optional)
2 tbsp. butter   ½ cup green onions
2 tbsp. flour   ¼ cup bread crumbs
1 cup milk   1 tbsp. grated cheese
½ tsp. salt
¼ tsp. pepper

- Do not break flowerets from main stem. Rinse and trim off any dark spots. Steam for approximately 15 minutes.
- Drain and place in baking dish.
- Melt butter in small skillet, add flour and stir. Add milk and stir until smooth and thick.
- Add salt, pepper, pimiento and onions.
- Pour over cauliflower and top with bread crumbs and cheese.
- Bake for 20 minutes.

Maple Glazed Carrots
(Serves 4)

½ lb. fresh baby carrots or carrot sticks   3 tbsp. maple syrup
2 tbsp. butter

- Cook carrots and drain well.
- Spoon butter and maple syrup over carrots in the pan.
- Return carrots to heat and toss them in glazing liquid until well coated.
- Serve in warmed serving dish.

Maple Butter Tarts
(Yields 12 medium tarts, Oven 375°)

pastry for 12 medium tarts (see Basics, page 212)
½ cup raisins
¼ cup butter
½ cup brown sugar
¼ tsp. salt

½ cup maple syrup
1 egg, beaten
½ tsp. vanilla
lemon juice

- Pour boiling water over raisins and let soak. Drain.
- Cream butter and add sugar. Beat well.
- Add salt, maple syrup, egg, vanilla and a few drops of lemon juice.
- Add drained raisins. Spoon into unbaked tart shells.
- Bake for 15 to 20 minutes.

_____ For The Sweet Tooth _____

Eggs Poached in Maple Syrup
(Serves 2)

1 cup maple syrup

2 eggs

- Place maple syrup in a saucepan and bring to a boil.
- Break each egg onto a separate saucer and slip eggs into hot syrup. Simmer 3 to 5 minutes. Spoon hot syrup over eggs as they cook.
- Serve hot in cereal bowl with hot buttered toast.

Café Brûlot
(Serves 6-8)

peel of 1 orange, thinly cut
4 sticks cinnamon
10 whole cloves

¼ cup maple syrup
½ cup brandy
4 cups prepared hot coffee

- Place peel, spices and maple syrup in a chafing dish.
- Heat brandy. Ignite and pour over other ingredients in bowl.
- Gradually add hot coffee and ladle mixture until flame dies. Serve immediately.

Maple Butter

½ cup maple sugar

¼ cup unsalted butter

- Cream together until smooth. Serve on hot toast.

Maple Cream

1 cup maple sugar   2 tbsp. whipping cream

- Combine maple sugar and whipping cream in a saucepan. Cook over medium heat stirring constantly until sugar is dissolved and mixture begins to boil. Cook to soft ball (238°F). Let cool to lukewarm and a pale golden colour.
- Pour into a well buttered cake pan. Cut into serving pieces when set.

Double Crust Maple Sugar Pie

(Yields one 9″ pie, Oven 450°)

pastry for 9″ double crust pie   ¼ tsp. salt
  (see Basics, page 212)   ¼ tsp. nutmeg
1 cup maple sugar   4 tsp. flour
1¼ cups milk
1 egg, beaten
2 tbsp. butter

- Line pie plate with pastry.
- Combine ingredients in top half of double boiler and cook until thickened. Cool.
- Pour into prepared, unbaked pie shell. Place upper crust over filling. Bake at 450° for 10 minutes. Reduce heat to 350° and bake additional 20 minutes, until brown.

Preparation Note: Bake on rack below centre of oven to allow bottom pastry to bake properly.

Single Crust Maple Sugar Pie

(Yields one 9″ pie, Oven 450°)

pastry for single crust 9″ pie   2 eggs, beaten
  (see Basics, page 212)   1 tbsp. butter
1¼ cups maple sugar   1 cup whipping cream, whipped
¾ cup whipping cream

- Line pie plate with pastry.
- Combine all ingredients except 1 cup whipping cream in top half of double boiler and cook until thickened. Cool.
- Pour into pie shell and bake 450° for 10 minutes. Reduce to 350° and bake an additional 50 minutes. Cool. Serve topped with whipped cream.

Maple Syrup Pie

(Yields one 9″ pie, Oven 400°)

pastry for one 9″ double crust pie shell   1 cup maple syrup
  (see Basics, page 212)   1 tbsp. butter
3 tbsp. cornstarch
5 oz. water

- Dissolve cornstarch in 2 tablespoons of water.
- Combine ingredients in a saucepan and boil until transparent. Cool.
- Pour into unbaked pie crust. Put top pastry in place and bake 30 minutes. Bake on rack below centre of oven.

Maple Baked Apples
(Serves 8, Oven 375°)

8 medium sized Granny Smith apples   8 tbsp. raisins
½ cup hot water   8 tbsp. maple syrup

- Do not peel but core apples almost through so they will not leak.
- Place apples in a cake pan holding hot water.
- In each apple, place one tablespoon of raisins and maple syrup to fill cavity. Bake 30 minutes.

Maple Rice Pudding
(Serves 6-8, Oven 350°)

⅔ cup cooked rice   ⅓ cup raisins
2 eggs, beaten   ½ tsp. salt
1½ cups whole milk   ½ tsp. nutmeg
⅔ cup maple syrup

- Combine ingredients in a buttered 1 quart casserole and place in a pan of hot water.
- Bake 1 hour.

Substitute maple sugar or syrup in your favourite recipe as follows:

Maple Sugar: allow ½ cup of maple sugar for each cup of granulated sugar.

Maple Syrup: allow ¾ cup syrup for each cup of sugar. In baking, reduce other liquid called for by 3 tablespoons for every cup of syrup substituted.

After the Festival
(For 12)

Caesar Salad
Onion Rolls
Champlain Stew
Browned Rice
Baked Alaska au Canadian Cocktail

Caesar Salad
(Serves 12)

4 cloves garlic, peeled
1 cup olive oil
1½ cups cubed bread
2 large heads Romaine lettuce
    (approximately 6 cups)
3 tsp. salt
¾ tsp. dry mustard
½ tbsp. pepper

5 anchovy fillets, finely chopped
5 drops Worcestershire sauce
6 tbsp. wine vinegar
2 eggs, beaten
juice of 1 lemon
Parmesan cheese

- Slice 2 cloves of garlic and place in olive oil. Let garlic sit in oil for 24 hours.
- Sauté cubed bread in 4 tbsp. garlic oil.
- Wash and break lettuce into 2″ strips. Dry well.
- Rub salad bowl thoroughly with remaining two cloves of garlic. (Cut in half and rub bowl with cut edges.)
- Combine remaining garlic oil with next eight ingredients. Shake well.
- Place dressing on salad; sprinkle generously with Parmesan cheese.
- Place croutons on top and serve immediately.

Onion Rolls
(Yields 4 dozen, Oven 400°)

2 envelopes onion soup mix
3½ cups water
¼ cup sugar
¼ cup grated Parmesan cheese
1 tbsp. salt
2 tbsp. shortening
1 tsp. sugar

½ cup lukewarm water
¼ tsp. ginger
1 envelope dry yeast
8-9 cups flour
¾ cup finely chopped onions
3 tbsp. butter
½ cup grated Parmesan cheese

- Simmer onion soup mix in water, covered, for 10 minutes.
- Add sugar, cheese, salt and shortening. Stir until shortening melts. Cool to lukewarm.
- Dissolve 1 tsp. sugar in lukewarm water. Add ginger. Sprinkle yeast on water. Let stand 10 minutes.
- Stir well, and add to onion mixture in a large mixing bowl.
- Gradually add flour, mixing after each addition.
- Turn out on floured board and knead until smooth and elastic (8 to 10 minutes.)
- Shape into a smooth ball and place in greased bowl, rotating so entire surface is greased.
- Cover and set in a warm place to rise, about 1¼ hours or until doubled.
- Punch down and shape into rolls. (May also be prepared in two loaves).
- Place on greased pans.
- Cover. Let rise until double, about 45 minutes.
- Sauté chopped onions in butter.
- Sprinkle sautéed onions and grated Parmesan cheese over rolls.
- Bake for 25 to 35 minutes.

Champlain Stew
(Serves 12)

4 tbsp. flour
½ tsp. celery salt
½ tsp. ginger
½ tsp. garlic salt
¼ tsp. pepper
4 lbs. stewing beef, cut in 2″ cubes

3 tbsp. fat
1 can (16 oz.) stewed tomatoes
4 medium onions, sliced
⅓ cup red wine vinegar
¼ cup maple syrup
2 cups water
2 cups carrots, cut in 1″ diagonal pieces

- Mix flour, celery salt, ginger, garlic salt and pepper in a plastic bag.
- Place beef in bag, approximately 1 pound at a time and shake until meat is coated with flour mixture.
- In a heavy skillet, melt fat and brown meat in hot fat. Transfer to cooking kettle.
- Add tomatoes, onions, vinegar, maple syrup and water.
- Bring to a boil, cover and simmer 3 hours.
- Add carrots in the last hour of cooking.

Preparation Note: For a tasty touch, add a half cup of raisins in the last half hour of cooking.

Browned Rice
(Serves 10-12, Oven 300°)

½ cup butter
2 cups long grain rice
2 tsp. salt
¼ tsp. pepper

2 10oz. cans consommé
2 cups water
¾ cup blanched almonds, chopped

- In a large frying pan, melt butter over low heat. Add rice and cook until golden brown, stirring often.
- Place cooked rice in a 2 quart casserole and sprinkle on seasonings.
- Add consommé, water and nuts and mix gently.
- Cover casserole and bake for approximately 1 hour. Do not stir.

Baked Alaska au Canadian Cocktail*
(Serves 12)

*"Canadian Cocktail" is equal parts scotch and maple syrup. Best prepared a couple of weeks ahead and kept in the refrigerator.

12″ flan (double recipe Butter Sponge
   cake—see Basics, page 208)
½ cup Canadian Cocktail*

2 litres maple walnut ice cream
1 recipe Meringue (below)

- Prepare flan a day ahead of time, cover and set aside.
- Sprinkle cake with Canadian Cocktail*.
- Let ice cream soften slightly and spoon into a 10″ pie plate.
- Place in freezer until ready to assemble cake for serving.

Meringue:
9 egg whites   ½ cup sugar

- Beat egg whites until very frothy.
- Add sugar; continue beating until whites are stiff but not dry.

To Assemble:
- Invert ice cream onto cake and cover with Meringue so the cake surface is entirely coated.
- Place under broiler for about 3 minutes or until golden.
- Serve at once.

Serving Suggestion: Serve with a liqueur glass of Canadian Cocktail*.

Huronia Spring Pork
(For 8)
**Sherried Tomato Consommé
Pork Tenderloin en Croûte
Baked Tomatoes with Creamed Spinach
Carrots Vichy
Grapes Juanita
Pumpkin Bread**

Sherried Tomato Consommé
(Serves 8)

6 cups chicken broth
3 cups canned Italian tomatoes in juice
2 tbsp. sugar

salt and pepper to taste
½ cup medium dry sherry
chives or scallions for garnish

- Combine all ingredients except sherry and chives, bringing to a boil over moderately high heat. Reduce heat and simmer 15 minutes.
- Add sherry and heat; ladle into heated bowls.
- Garnish with thinly sliced scallions or chives.

Pork Tenderloin en Croûte
(Serves 8, Oven 400°)

2 1½ to 2 lb. tenderloins (3 to 4 lbs. total)
salt and pepper
1 tsp. sage
4 tbsp. butter
1 clove garlic, minced
2 cooking onions

4 cooking apples
1 cup mushrooms
2 lbs. pastry (see Basics, page 212 or
  frozen puff pastry)
8 oz. pâté
2 eggs, well beaten

- Trim away all fat from meat and divide into 8 portions. Season with salt, pepper and sage.
- Heat butter in frying pan; add garlic.
- Sear meat on all sides.
- Reduce heat and cook 20 to 30 minutes turning occasionally until fully cooked and nicely browned.
- Cool meat thoroughly.
- Chop onions, apples and mushrooms; sauté in butter and set aside.
- Roll out pastry and divide into 8 rectangles about 6½" x 10".
- Spread pâté on pastry and place piece of meat on top.
- Top each piece of meat with apple, onion and mushroom mixture. With pastry brush, brush egg along edges of pastry.
- Fold pastry over meat and apple, onion and mushroom mixture; press lightly to seal

edges. Set remaining egg aside.
- Keep refrigerated until ready to place in oven.
- About 35 minutes before serving, preheat oven.
- Add a little water to remaining egg and brush over pastry.
- Bake 30 minutes until golden.

Baked Tomatoes with Creamed Spinach
(Serves 8, Oven 375°)

8 medium sized tomatoes
salt
2 lbs. spinach
3 oz. butter
1 tbsp. butter
1 tbsp. flour

¾ cup milk
¾ cup whipping cream
salt, pepper and nutmeg to taste
1 recipe Creamed Spinach (below)

Tomatoes
- Core tomatoes, removing centre and some pulp, leaving a thick shell.
- Sprinkle with salt.
- Invert on a wire rack for 1 hour.

Creamed Spinach
- Clean spinach and steam for 6 minutes.
- Rinse with cold water, drain well and chop fine.
- Melt 3 oz. of butter in pan and add chopped spinach.
- Heat until moisture has evaporated.
- In separate saucepan, melt 1 tbsp. butter and stir in flour.
- Slowly stir in milk and continue to cook until thickened.
- Add the white sauce and heavy cream to spinach.
- Simmer mixture until reduced to desired consistency.
- Season to taste with salt, pepper and nutmeg.

To Assemble
- In a buttered baking dish, arrange tomatoes right side up.
- Place ½ tsp. butter in each tomato.
- Heat for 10 minutes in oven.
- Remove from oven and fill with spinach mixture.
- Return to oven and cook for 5 minutes.

Carrots Vichy
(Serves 8)

2 lbs. carrots
½ lb. butter
1 tsp. salt

1 tsp. icing sugar
2 oz. brandy

- Peel carrots and cut into very thin slices.
- Melt butter in heavy pan; season with salt and sugar.
- Add carrots and brandy.
- Cover and continue to cook over low heat for 1 hour or until done. Do not stir except to test for doneness. The carrots will have absorbed all the butter and will not be dry.

Preparation Note: Can be prepared in advance and reheated.

Grapes Juanita
(Serves 8)

4 lbs. seedless grapes
2 cups sour cream

1 cup brown sugar

- Combine grapes and sour cream.
- Sprinkle brown sugar on top.
- Chill at least 2 hours before serving and serve in stemmed glasses.

Serving Suggestion: Nice served with Camembert cheese.

Pumpkin Bread
(Yields 9″ x 5″ loaf, Oven 350°)

⅓ cup shortening
1½ cup sugar
2 eggs
1 cup prepared pumpkin
1¾ cup flour
1 tsp. salt

¼ tsp. baking powder
½ tsp. cloves
1 tsp. baking soda
½ tsp. cinnamon
⅓ cup orange juice

- Cream first three ingredients and add pumpkin. Mix well.
- Sift dry ingredients and add alternately with orange juice to pumpkin mixture.
- Bake in 9″ x 5″ x 3″ pan 45 to 60 minutes.
- Cool in pan 10 minutes before removing.

Preparation Note: You may add chopped walnuts and/or raisins according to your preference.

MENU

Ladies' Spring Luncheon
(For 6)
Cold Sour Cherry Soup
Quiche Florentine
Crunchy Vegetable Salad
Tortoni
Very Best Brownies

Cold Sour Cherry Soup
(Serves 6)

1¼ pints cold water
½ lb. brown sugar
1 cinnamon stick
1 lb. pitted sour cherries or drained
   tinned sour cherries

1 tbsp. arrowroot
2 tbsp. cold water
3 tbsp. heavy cream, chilled
6 oz. dry red wine, chilled

- In a saucepan, combine water, sugar and cinnamon stick. Bring to a boil and add cherries.
- Partially cover and simmer over low heat for 35 to 40 minutes if the cherries are fresh, or for 10 minutes if they are canned.
- Remove the cinnamon stick.
- Mix arrowroot and 2 tbsp. of cold water into a paste, then mix into the cherry soup. Stirring constantly, bring mixture almost to the boil.
- Reduce heat and simmer for 2 minutes or until clear and slightly thickened.
- Pour into a glass or stainless steel bowl and refrigerate until chilled.
- Just prior to serving, stir in cream and wine.

Quiche Florentine
(Serves 6, Oven 325°)

pastry for 11" quiche pan (see Basics,
   page 212)
8 oz. frozen chopped spinach
⅓ cup butter
4 oz. cottage or cream cheese

salt, pepper and nutmeg to taste
2 eggs
1-2 oz. grated Parmesan cheese
canned red pimiento, cut into strips

- Line an 11" quiche pan or pie plate with pastry. Prick bottom and bake 10 minutes at 400°.
- Steam spinach 6 minutes. Drain, add butter and toss with spinach.
- Mix in cottage cheese or cream cheese. Season with salt, pepper and nutmeg.
- Beat eggs and add to spinach mixture.
- Turn mixture into pie shell, smooth top and sprinkle with grated Parmesan cheese. Bake 20 minutes.
- Remove quiche from oven and decorate top with a criss-cross design of red pimiento.
- Return to oven for 20 minutes. Serve hot or cold.

Preparation Note: May also be made into individual tarts. Makes 10 tarts.

Crunchy Vegetable Salad
(Serves 6-8)

1 head cauliflower chopped into
  bite-sized pieces
1 cup radishes, thinly sliced
¼ cup green onions, chopped

1 8oz. can water chestnuts, sliced
1 recipe Dressing (below)

- Combine vegetables and water chestnuts in a medium sized bowl or container.
- Toss with Dressing. Cover and refrigerate.

Dressing:

1 cup mayonnaise
1 cup sour cream

1 pkg. dry salad seasoning: garlic-cheese
  dressing
4 tsp. caraway seeds

- Place ingredients in container and blend thoroughly. Cover and refrigerate.

Preparation Note: This salad is best made ahead. Stored in a covered container, it will keep for days.

Tortoni
(Serves 6)

1 pint vanilla ice cream
¼ cup chopped candied fruits and peels
¼ cup seedless raisins

¼ tsp. rum flavouring
6 maraschino cherries
30 whole toasted almonds

- Allow ice cream to soften slightly.
- Add candied fruits and peels, raisins and rum flavouring.
- Spoon into 6 paper baking cups set in muffin tins.
- Freeze until nearly firm.
- Top each serving with a maraschino cherry and poke in a circle of whole toasted almonds, point down.
- Freeze firm.
- Serve in paper cup, on a dessert plate.

Very Best Brownies
(Yields 12 brownies, Oven 350°)

1 egg
½ cup sugar
¼ cup butter
1½ heaping tbsp. cocoa

¼ cup flour
½ tsp. baking powder
½ cup chopped walnuts
3 oz. small raisins

- Beat eggs and sugar thoroughly.
- Melt butter and add cocoa.
- Combine flour and baking powder.
- Mix together all ingredients except nuts and raisins. (Mixture will be fairly stiff.)
- Fold in nuts and raisins.
- Spread mixture into a 7″ square tin, greased and floured.
- Bake for about 30 minutes.
- Cut into 12 oblong pieces and allow to partially cool before removing from tin.

Deerhurst

"Casual elegance and cozy fireplaces": that is how Deerhurst Inn has been described in the past, and we were fortunate enough to find that this Inn continues to live up to its fine reputation.

We had finished collecting and testing our recipes and needed to get away and cloister ourselves to pull the whole thing together and add the finishing touches. It was decided that the "Georgian Bay Gourmets" would treat themselves for Mother's Day; so we headed north to the Muskokas to work.

Deerhurst Inn and Country Club is 4 miles east of Huntsville on Peninsula Lake. It was indeed difficult to concentrate on our work with the whole myriad of activities there. We were unable to go boating or golfing or enjoy a game of tennis, however we did break for a swim and a whirlpool, and of course to enjoy "Chefy's" fine cuisine. We even managed to take in the Second City Revue one evening, and made a brief visit to the lively Disco situated next to the main lodge.

The staff at Deerhurst is very friendly and warm. Our hats off to "Chefy" who welcomed us into his kitchen and shared his recipes with us. In this section, our special feature is the recipe for his famous rice pudding!

We highly recommend Deerhurst Inn where one finds out that it is not always necessary to travel south for excellent accommodations, superb food, a wide range of activities, and good times. Try it—you'll like it!

Chefy's Rice Pudding
(Serves 20, Oven 350°)

2½ cups long grain rice
3 quarts half and half cream
12 eggs, beaten
2½ cups sugar

4 tsp. vanilla
2½ cups raisins

- Cook rice according to package directions.
- Scald cream.
- Combine eggs, sugar, and vanilla.
- Place rice and raisins in oven proof casserole; add cream and egg mixture. Stir.
- Place casserole in a pan of hot water and bake until custard is partially set (approximately 30 minutes).
- Remove from oven. Stir and set aside to cool.

Basics

Hollandaise Sauce
(Yields 1½ cups)

¾ cup unsalted butter   ¼ tsp. salt
4 egg yolks   dash of white pepper
1 tbsp. cold water   1 tsp. lemon juice

- Melt butter in a saucepan. Remove from heat and skim off foam.
- Place egg yolks and water in top of a double boiler or heavy enamel pan. Beat yolks and water continuously with a wire whisk until they have formed a thick custard.
- Gradually add butter, beating constantly.
- Season with salt, pepper and lemon juice.

Preparation Note: To cure curdled Hollandaise, beat an egg yolk with ¼ tsp. dry mustard. Gradually add the curdled mixture to the fresh yolk.

White Cream Sauce—Béchamel
(Yields 2 cups)

4 tbsp. butter   ½ tsp. salt
4 tbsp. flour   ⅛ tsp. white pepper
2 cups cold milk or cream   1 tsp. sugar

- Melt butter in skillet.
- Add flour and cook, stirring constantly for 3 minutes. Do not allow to brown.
- Add cold milk and seasonings including sugar. Cook, stirring constantly, until thickened.

Auntie Vin's Super Yummy Mayonnaise
(Yields 2 pints)

½ cup water   1 tsp. dry mustard
2 cups white vinegar   2 cups sugar
½ cup flour   2 eggs, beaten

- Place water and vinegar in a saucepan and bring to a boil. Boil for a few minutes.
- Mix flour, mustard, sugar and eggs.
- Pour hot vinegar mixture slowly over egg mixture and stir.
- Place in a double boiler, cook, stirring constantly, until thick.

Preparation Note: Mixture is quite thick. Refrigerate and thin to desired consistency with thick cream as you use it.

Crême Fraîche
1½ tsp. buttermilk   1 cup whipping cream

- Combine ingredients in a sterilized jar and shake well.
- Loosen lid and set out on countertop at room temperature for 8 hours.
- Tighten lid, shake again and refrigerate.

Preparation Note: This will keep up to 10 days in refrigerator.

Basic Stocks

Beef Stock

3 lbs. beef bones

1½ lbs. lean beef

2 leeks

3-4 carrots

3-4 stalks celery

2 whole cloves

2 cooking onions

3 quarts cold water

- Put bones and meat into a large kettle.
- Clean vegetables.
- Fold greens of leeks over whites and tie in a bundle.
- Cut carrots in quarters.
- Cut celery in quarters. Use tops as well.
- Stuff cloves into one onion.
- Put vegetables in kettle with meat and cover with water.
- Simmer for 3 hours and then strain broth.

Chicken Broth

Substitute 1 2 to 3 lb. frying chicken for the bones and meat in above recipe.

Canned Stocks

Improve the flavour of canned stocks to use in your favourite recipe by simmering carrots, parsley, onions or any other vegetables in the broth for approximately 20 minutes. Strain and use.

Consommé

(Yields approximately 6 cups)

Consommé means perfectly refined soup and is made from clarified stock.

To Clarify Stock:

½ cup cold water

4 egg whites

6 cups stock, well seasoned

salt and pepper

red or brown food colouring for beef
  stock (optional)

2 tbsp. Madeira

1 tbsp. cognac

- Place water and egg whites in a saucepan and beat to a froth. Pour in cold stock and season with salt and pepper.
- Bring to a boil, stirring constantly. When mixture reaches the boil, reduce heat, stop stirring, and let simmer 10 minutes (do not let it bubble; the egg whites will absorb the impurities in the stock).
- Pour liquid through a clean damp linen cloth, being careful not to break up cooked egg whites.
- If working with beef stock, add food colouring. Add Madeira and cognac.

Preparation Note: If stock has a lot of impurities, add more egg whites. It should never require more than 1 egg white per cup of stock. It's best to start with well seasoned, fairly concentrated stock.

con't

Jellied Consommé

To jelly consommé, dissolve 1½ tsp. gelatin for every 2 cups hot consommé and refrigerate for 4 hours.

Butter Sponge Cake

(Yields 10″ round cake, Oven 350°)

3 tbsp. butter
4 eggs
7 tbsp. sugar + 3 tbsp. sugar

½ tsp. vanilla
⅔ cup flour

- Melt butter and put aside. Do not let it get cooler than 80°F.
- Place a mixing bowl or top half of double boiler over pan of hot, not boiling, water. Water is not to touch bowl or top half of double boiler.
- In bowl, place eggs and heat until lukewarm.
- Add 7 tbsp. sugar. Beat with an electric mixer at medium speed for 7 minutes.
- Add 3 tbsp. sugar. Increase mixer speed and beat for 2 minutes longer. Mixture should be lemony in colour and stand in soft peaks. It should be about triple in volume.
- Add vanilla.
- Fold in flour and melted butter.
- Pour batter into ungreased pan and bake 40 minutes or until done. Turn cake out onto a rack at once to cool.

Preparation Note: This is a one bowl cake you'll love to make. It is an airy sponge cake that does just about anything you would want a basic cake to do. It is great for Baked Alaskas, Strawberry Shortcake, roll cakes with cream fillings; also sliced into layers and slathered with butter cream frostings or as a back drop for fruit in a flan.

Basic White Cake

(Yields 9″ layer, Oven 350°)

1½ cups flour
2½ tsp. baking powder
½ tsp. salt
¾ cup sugar

⅓ cup shortening, melted, or
     vegetable oil
¾ cup milk
2 eggs

- Into a large bowl, sift dry ingredients. Add shortening and milk and beat for 1 minute with electric mixer on low.
- Add eggs and beat an additional 2 minutes on low speed.
- Coat cake pan with shortening and oil and dust with flour.
- Pour batter into prepared pan. Bake 40 to 45 minutes or until cake springs back when lightly touched.

Overnight Rolls
(Yields 6 dozen, Oven 375°)

This is great for the working person or to surprise guests with fresh homemade rolls for brunch.

4 cups lukewarm water	1 cup vegetable oil
¾ cup sugar	1 tbsp. salt
¼ tsp. ginger	1 egg
1 pkg. yeast	12-12½ cups flour

5 or 6 p.m.:
- In a small bowl combine 1 cup of the lukewarm water, 2 tsp. sugar and the ginger. Sprinkle on yeast and let stand for 10 minutes. Mix with a fork once it is foamy.
- Combine remaining 3 cups water, sugar, oil, salt, and egg.
- Add yeast mixture.
- Gradually add flour. Place on a floured surface and knead until smooth (approximately 10 minutes).
- Place dough in a well greased bowl. Cover and let rise until doubled (approximately 2 hours).

8 or 9 p.m.:
- Punch down and allow to rise an additional 90 minutes.

9:30 - 10:00 p.m.:
- Shape as desired (ie. pan rolls, Parkerhouse, cloverleaf etc.). Place on greased pans, cover with clean tea towel and let rise overnight.

a.m.:
- Bake 15 minutes or until golden; cool on cooling racks.

Preparation Note: These rolls freeze well and can be pulled out at the last minute, dressed up with butter and herbs, cheese etc. and served with any menu. If being prepared to freeze, bake a few minutes less.

Mom's Dinner Rolls
(Yields 2 dozen, Oven 400°)

1 cup milk	2 tbsp. soft butter
2 tbsp. sugar	1 tsp. salt
⅓ cup lukewarm water	2½ cups flour
1 pkg. yeast	

- Scald milk and cool to lukewarm.
- In a small bowl dissolve sugar in lukewarm water.
- Add yeast; stir and let stand 10 minutes.
- Combine yeast mixture, milk, butter, salt and 1 cup flour. Beat until smooth. Gradually add remaining flour to make a soft dough.
- Turn out onto lightly floured board and knead until smooth and elastic (approximately 10 minutes).
- Place in a greased bowl. Cover and let rise in a warm place until double in size (approximately 1½ hours).
- Punch down and cut into 24 pieces. Shape rolls into desired shape.
- Place on greased baking sheet. Cover and let rise until double in bulk (approximately 1 hour).
- Bake 10 to 12 minutes.

Basic White Bread
(Yields 4 loaves, Oven 400°)

2 cups milk
3 tbsp. + 2 tsp. sugar
4 tsp. salt
¼ cup shortening
1 cup 2% or skim milk

1 cup lukewarm water
¼ tsp. ginger
2 tbsp. (2 envelopes) active dry yeast
10 cups flour

- Scald 2 cups of milk.
- Pour into a large bowl and add 3 tbsp. sugar, salt, shortening and milk. Stir until shortening melts. Cool to lukewarm.
- Meanwhile dissolve 2 tsp. sugar in lukewarm water (100°F-105°F). Add ginger. Sprinkle active dry yeast over this. Let stand for 10 minutes, then stir briskly with a fork.
- Add softened yeast to lukewarm milk mixture. Stir.
- With electric mixer, beat in 5 cups of flour.
- With a spoon, gradually beat in an additional 4½ to 5 cups of flour. Last of flour may have to be worked in by hand.
- Turn dough onto a floured surface and knead approximately 10 minutes. Dough is kneaded enough when surface is smooth and satiny, and looks stretched. Dough should feel springy and elastic to touch.
- Shape into a smooth ball and place in greased bowl, rotating dough to grease surface. Cover with a damp cloth. Place in a warm draft-free space, and let rise until doubled (about 1½ hours).
- Punch down. Allowing bread to rise a second time before shaping is not necessary but makes for a much lighter textured bread. Second rising should take about 1 hour. Punch down and shape into four loaves.
- To form loaves, cut dough in four equal portions. On a floured surface roll one ball of dough into a rectangle measuring 8″ wide and 10″ long. Press out large air bubbles.
- Starting on the long side, fold both ends into the middle. Press out trapped air bubbles. Seal by pressing edges with fingers. Stretch width of dough slightly. Repeat procedures on all four loaves.
- Place in lightly greased 8½″ x 4½″ bread pans. Brush tops of loaves with melted butter or shortening. Cover and let rise until double (about 1 hour).
- Bake 30 to 35 minutes.

Whole Wheat Bread
(Yields 2 loaves, Oven 425°)

1½ cups hot tap water
½ cup instant powdered milk
1 tbsp. molasses
1 tbsp. honey
2 tsp. salt
1 tsp. sugar
⅛ tsp. ginger

½ cup warm water
1 pkg. yeast
2 cups whole wheat flour, or 1 cup whole
    wheat flour and 1 cup graham flour
¼ cup wheat germ
2 tbsp. soft butter
2-2½ cups white flour

- In a large bowl, mix the hot water, milk powder, molasses, honey and salt.
- In a small bowl, stir the sugar, ginger and warm water. Sprinkle yeast on top. Let both mixtures stand 10 minutes; stir and combine.

- Add wholewheat flour and wheat germ and beat well. Add butter and mix in. Add white flour.
- Turn dough out on floured board and knead for 8 to 10 minutes.
- Place in greased bowl, cover with cloth and let rise 1 hour or until doubled in bulk.
- Punch down and knead 30 seconds. Divide and shape into 2 loaves. Cover and let rise until double (approximately 1 hour).
- Bake at 425° for 15 minutes and then reduce heat to 350° for 15 minutes.

Tea Biscuit Mix

This is great to have on hand to make biscuits, pancakes or muffins.

5 cups flour
3 tbsp. baking powder
1 tbsp. sugar

½ tsp. salt
1 cup shortening

- Combine dry ingredients.
- Cut in shortening with a pastry blender until mixture resembles coarse crumbs.
- Store in a covered container. Will keep up to 6 weeks at room temperature. Will keep longer if refrigerated but allow to come to room temperature before using.

To Make Biscuits
(Yields 10 biscuits, Oven 450°)

2 cups biscuit mix (above)   ½ cup milk

- Place mix in bowl and add milk. Stir with a fork to make soft dough.
- Turn dough onto lightly floured surface and knead gently 8 to 10 times.
- Roll or pat to desired thickness. (Biscuits will double in height when baked).
- Cut with a 2½″ floured cutter. Place on a greased baking sheet and bake 10 to 12 minutes.

To Make Pancakes
(Yields 10 pancakes)

1⅓ cups milk
1 egg, beaten

2 cups biscuit mix (above)

- Combine milk and egg. Add mix and beat until smooth.
- Cook on lightly greased skillet.

To Make Muffins
(Yields 12 muffins, Oven 400°)

1 cup milk
1 egg, beaten
3 cups biscuit mix (above)

2 tbsp. sugar
½ cup raisins, blueberries or other fruit

- Combine ingredients and stir to moisten.
- Fill greased muffin tins ⅔'s full. Bake 20 to 25 minutes.

Never Fail Pastry
(Yields 3 double pie crusts)

This is a great pastry recipe. It never fails and keeps 2 to 3 weeks in the refrigerator. Frozen, it will last up to 6 months.

5 cups flour	1 lb. shortening
½ tsp. soda	1 egg, beaten
2 tsp. sugar	3 tbsp. lemon juice or white vinegar
2 tsp. salt	iced water

- Place flour, soda, sugar and salt in a large bowl and stir.
- Add shortening. With 2 knives or a pastry blender, cut in shortening.
- In a 1 cup measure, combine 1 egg and lemon juice (or vinegar).
- Add iced water to fill cup.
- Pour liquid over flour mixture. Mix with a fork until a ball starts to form in the bowl. Turn onto a generously floured board, knead and turn mixture until it shapes into a ball. Wrap tightly in plastic wrap. Refrigerate at least one hour before using.
- To roll out to a well shaped circle, shape dough into a round disc, flat on top and bottom. Shape edges smoothly. Roll pastry, always starting at centre of dough and rolling to outside edges. Vary starting position of rolling pin and direction of roll to cover complete section. Pastry should be about 1″ larger than inverted pie plate. For best results, roll out pastry dough on canvas cloth with rolling pin covered in stockinette. The strands of cloth hold flour to prevent dough from sticking and added flour is not worked in.

Preparation Note: Lard and shortening are interchangeable. It is a matter of personal preference. Experiment with each or a combination of each. Butter may also be substituted for a portion of the fat.

Baked Pie Shell
(Oven 400°)

- Fit dough loosely in pie plate. Trim ½″ beyond edge and fold under. Flute edge of pastry.
- Prick at 1″ intervals. Bake 10 to 12 minutes until golden brown. Cool before adding cooked filling.

Unbaked Pie Shell

- Prepare as above, but do not prick. Add uncooked filling and bake as directed in recipe.
- Place oven rack slightly lower than centre to allow bottom of pie to bake.

Double Crust Pie

- Add filling to lined pie plate and moisten edges.
- Roll out top crust and place on filled pie.
- Trim off excess pastry, seal edges and flute.
- Make slits in centre to allow steam to escape. Bake as above.

Pastry

Single 8″ or 9″ crust

1½ cups flour

½ tsp. salt

½ cup shortening

4-5 tbsp. ice cold water

Double 8″ or 9″ crust

2 cups flour

1 tsp. salt

¾ cup shortening

5-6 tbsp. ice cold water

- In a medium sized bowl, combine flour and salt.
- Add shortening and cut in with a pastry blender until it is the consistency of coarse meal with a few larger pieces.
- Add water, 1 tablespoon at a time. Mix lightly with a fork until dough clings together when pinched with fingers. Form into a ball. Chill until ready to use.
- To line pie plate, use a lightly floured surface to roll out to ⅛″ thickness.

Preparation Note: Read instructions and tips for Never Fail Pastry. The same principles apply.

Vegetables

Some general notes about preparing vegetables:

- Vegetables should be peeled (as thinly as possible) or scrubbed until thoroughly clean.
- Leave vegetables whole or cut them in fairly large pieces to preserve food values and flavour.
- Cook only until just tender. Overcooking reduces food values, and destroys colour and flavour.
- Add prepared vegetables to a small amount of vigorously boiling water (½ to 1" deep). Cover tightly. When water returns to the boil, reduce heat to keep water boiling gently.

    Whole potatoes and beets require a little more water; leafy green vegetables will cook (over moderate heat) in the water which clings to the washed leaves.

Vegetable Chart

Vegetable	Amount to Purchase for 4	Preparation	Boiling Time (Minutes)
Asparagus	2½ lbs.	Cut off tough ends. Peel stalk with a potato peeler. Stand in a tall saucepan or coffee pot. Add 2" depth of boiling salted water. Cook covered.	5-15
Beans Green & Waxed	1 lb.	Wash. Snip off ends. Cut in 1" pieces or leave whole.	15-25
Beets	2 lbs.	Cut off tops and root. Scrub well. Cover in salted boiling water. Remove skin after cooking.	40-60
Broccoli	2 lbs.	Remove outer leaves and tough part of stalk. Divide stalks into thumb sized stalks. Wash. Place in 1" boiling salted water. Cover and cook.	8-15
Brussels Sprouts	1½ lbs.	Remove tough and yellow bottom leaves. Cut each stem even with base. Cut a cross in the base of each stem.	8-15
Cabbage	1½ lbs.	Remove wilted outer leaves. Cut into 6 to 8 wedges.	10-12
		or Shredded. Cook in small amount of boiling salted water.	5-10
Carrots	1½ lbs.	Scrub, scrape or thinly pare. Small, whole	20-30
		Halved or quartered	15-20
		Thin strips or slices	10-15

Vegetable Chart

Vegetable	Amount to Purchase for 4	Preparation	Boiling Time (Minutes)
Cauliflower	2 lbs.	Remove outer leaves. Cut off any blemishes. Wash and cut out centre core.	
		Whole	20-30
		Flowerets	8-15
Celery	⅔ cup per serving	Remove leaves. Trim roots. Clean thoroughly. Cut in 1″ pieces.	15-20
Onions	1¾ lbs.	Trim ends and peel skins	
		Whole (2″ or larger)	30-35
		Whole (small)	20-35
		Slices (¼-½″)	10
Parsnips	1½ lbs.	Wash and pare. Cut into halves or quarters.	20-30
		Sliced or diced.	8-15
Peas, Green	3 lbs. in pod	Shell and wash. When ready to cook, add teaspoon of sugar to water.	8-15
Potatoes	1½ lb.	Scrub well. Remove blemishes Cook in skins or pare.	
		Whole	30-45
		Cut in halves or quarters	20-25
Spinach and greens	2 lbs.	Discard ends, tough stalks and yellow leaves. Wash several times in warm water. There should be enough water clinging to leaves to cook without adding additional water.	
		Spinach	5-10
		Beet tops	5-15
		Swiss chard	3-10
Squash	SUMMER 1½ lbs.	Scrub and remove ends. Cut into thin slices. Cook in ½″ boiling salted water.	15-20
	WINTER 2½ lbs.	Scrub well. Cut in half lengthwise.	25-30
		Remove seeds and stringy portion. Bake 350°.	40-60
Tomatoes	2 lbs.	Wash, pare thinly or scald and take off skins. Quarter and cook without water.	5-10
Turnips	1¾ lbs.	Scrub and pare. Slice or cube.	
		Whole	20-30
		Cut up	15-20

Georgian Bay Gourmets' Terms

BAKE: to cook by dry heat in oven.

BASTE: to spoon or brush liquid over food during cooking.

BEAT: to make a mixture smooth or introduce air by using a brisk regular motion that lifts the mixture over and over with a spoon or electric mixer.

BREAD: to coat with bread crumbs or cracker crumbs before cooking.

CARAMELIZE: to melt sugar over low heat until it becomes a brown liquid.

CHOP, DICE or MINCE: chopped = ¼" cubes; diced = ⅛" cubes; mince = 1/16" cubes.

CREAM: to blend ingredients until mixture becomes soft and fluffy.

DREDGE: to cover food evenly and generously with flour or other dry ingredient.

DUST: to lightly sprinkle food with flour or sugar or dry ingredient.

FOLD: to add a new ingredient to a mixture that has been beaten until light. The purpose is to add new ingredients without losing any of the air. Do this with the least amount of strokes.

FRY: to cook in hot fat: (a) pan frying calls for a little fat in pan, (b) deep frying is to immerse and cook food in deep fat.

GLAZE: to cover with a thin icing or a film of syrup or sugar.

KNEAD: a folding over and pressing together of dough to make it more elastic. Lift one half of dough with fingertips and fold over to give double thickness, then press together with heel of hand. Give dough a quarter turn and repeat.

MARINATE: to allow a food to stand for a time in a flavourful liquid to tenderize and/or add flavour.

MIX: to combine ingredients usually by stirring to produce an even distribution.

OVEN TEMPERATURE: oven heat usually stated at top of recipe and most often oven is preheated before food is placed inside.

PARBOIL: to boil until only partially cooked.

POACH: to cook in gently simmering liquid.

PROCESS: to combine two or more ingredients until well mixed, usually done in food processor or blender.

PURÉE: to place food in a food processor or blender or through a fine sieve until a thick smooth paste is formed.

SAUTÉ: to cook in an open pan with a small amount of fat on an even heat from start to finish. Food is to be seared in a rapid manner.

SCALD: to cook just below boiling point; tiny bubbles will form around the edge of the pan but not across surface of liquid.

SIMMER: to cook over gentle heat until bubbles come gently to the surface and barely seem to break.

STEAM: to cook food in a covered perforated container set over a small amount of boiling water.

STEW: to simmer for a long time in liquid.

STIR FRY: a method typical to Oriental cooking. This allows vegetables to remain tender, crisp and a very good colour. The cooking container must be very hot and contain oil. The vegetables or meat requiring most time go in first and the tenderest ones later so all is done at the same time. Stir frying usually takes only 3 to 4 minutes.

TOSS: to mix ingredients lightly.

WHIP: to beat rapidly to produce expansion by incorporating air as in heavy cream or egg whites.

Index

Desserts

Hors D'oeuvres, Canapés & Appetizers

Main Dishes
Meat, Seafood, Poultry & Casseroles

Sandwiches

Soups

Vegetables